Acting Edition

Cluedo

BASED ON THE SCREENPLAY BY
JONATHAN LYNN

WRITTEN BY
SANDY RUSTIN
ADDITIONAL MATERIAL BY
HUNTER FOSTER AND ERIC PRICE

BASED ON THE PARAMOUNT PICTURES MOTION PICTURE
BASED ON THE HASBRO BOARD GAME CLUEDO
WITH ADDITIONAL MATERIAL BY **MARK BELL**

DRAMATISTS PLAY SERVICE

Copyright © 2024, Clue Onstage LLC

CLUEDO and all related trademarks and logos are trademarks of Hasbro, Inc. Copyright © 2024, Hasbro.

All Rights Reserved

CLUEDO is fully protected under the copyright laws of the British Commonwealth, including Canada, the United States of America, and all other countries of the Copyright Union. All rights, including professional and amateur stage productions, recitation, lecturing, public reading, motion picture, radio broadcasting, television, online/digital production, and the rights of translation into foreign languages are strictly reserved.

ISBN 978-0-8222-4483-7

dramatists.com

concordtheatricals.co.uk

FOR PRODUCTION ENQUIRIES

UNITED KINGDOM AND WORLD
EXCLUDING NORTH AMERICA

licensing@concordtheatricals.co.uk

020-7054-7298

Each title is subject to availability from Concord Theatricals Corp., depending upon country of performance. Please be aware that *CLUEDO* may not be licensed by Concord Theatricals Corp. in your territory. Professional and amateur producers should contact the nearest Concord Theatricals Corp. office or licensing partner to verify availability.

CAUTION: Professional and amateur producers are hereby warned that *CLUEDO* is subject to a licensing fee. The purchase, renting, lending or use of this book does not constitute a license to perform this title(s), which license must be obtained from the appropriate agent prior to any performance. Performance of this title(s) without a license is a violation of copyright law and may subject the producer and/or presenter of such performances to penalties. Both amateurs and professionals considering a production are strongly advised to apply to the appropriate agent before starting rehearsals, advertising, or booking a theatre. A licensing fee must be paid whether the title is presented for charity or gain and whether or not admission is charged.

This work is published by Dramatists Play Service, an imprint of Concord Theatricals Corp.

For all inquiries regarding motion picture, television, online/digital and other media rights, please contact Dramatists Play Service, an imprint of Concord Theatricals Corp.

Please refer to the back of this volume for further copyright information.

Cast of Characters

WADSWORTH, a traditional butler in every sense: uptight, formal and 'by the book.' He is the driving force in the play.

YVETTE, a loyal and sexy 'French' maid.

MISS SCARLETT, a dry, sardonic madam, more interested in secrets than sex.

MRS PEACOCK, the wealthy wife of a member of the House of Lords. A bit batty, neurotic, and quick to hysteria.

MRS WHITE, a pale, morbid, and tragic woman. Mrs White may or may not be the murderer of her five ex-husbands.

COLONEL MUSTARD, a puffy, pompous, dense blowhard of a military man.

PROFESSOR PLUM, an arrogant academic, easily impressed by himself.

REVEREND GREEN, a timid yet officious rule follower. He's awfully anxious.

ENSEMBLE WOMAN:
    THE COOK, a gruff woman with a threatening presence. (Alive and Dead.)
    SINGING TELEGRAM GIRL, a tap dancer with a heart of gold. (Alive and Dead.)
    AUXILIARY SCARLETT, the back of Miss Scarlett during a scene of theatrical trickery.
    BACKUP OFFICER, backup for the Inspector in the very final police entrance.

ENSEMBLE MAN 1:
    MR. BODDY, a slick, Frank Sinatra, film noir-esque type fella. (Alive and Dead.)
    THE MOTORIST, a professional driver. (Alive and Dead.)
    INSPECTOR, a cop who helps to save the day.

ENSEMBLE MAN 2:
    BOBBY, a regular Joe. (Alive and Dead.)
    BACKUP OFFICER, backup for the Inspector.
    AUXILIARY MUSTARD, the back of Colonel Mustard during a scene of theatrical trickery.

PLEASE NOTE: An additional body to play the DEAD MOTORIST in the Lounge during Scene 11 is required. Perhaps an understudy or ASM can fill in for this 60-second moment of comedic razzle-dazzle.

Time

The play begins just before dinner on a dark and stormy night not too far from London, in 1949.

Place

Boddy Manor. A mansion of epic proportions and terrifying secrets.

Set

The interior of Boddy Manor. A grand hallway of a large, imposing, Gothic Victorian house, gloomy and menacing, is the focal point of the play. Doors that lead to the Library, the Study, the Lounge, the Billiard Room, the Conservatory, the Ballroom, the Kitchen, and the Dining Room line the Hall. The set is such that the various rooms of Boddy Manor easily pull out/appear in surprising ways, making transitions from one area of the house to another very fast.

Production Notes

Cluedo is a highly stylised ensemble piece. It is to be played with honesty and truth. The 'life or death' stakes of the situation are more important than comic bits. The pacing of *Cluedo* is intended to be very swift. This script maps out suggested physicality in some cases, but casts are encouraged to embrace the style and find their own moments of comedic physicality, while maintaining a truthful intention throughout.

Please note: UNO WHO should be pronounced 'You Know Who.'

Please note: The play takes place in the difficult post-war years in Britain. Rationing had been worse than during the war and people were fed up of austerity. Also, many people had done things during wartime that they now sought to hide. Everyone had secrets. Some highly placed people had been caught out by the Lynskey Tribunal (published in January 1949) breaking rationing rules and taking bribes, the press and the public were outraged. And demanded blood.

CLUEDO

Based on the screenplay by Jonathan Lynn
Written by Sandy Rustin

Additional Material by Hunter Foster and Eric Price
Based on the Paramount Pictures Motion Picture
Based on the Hasbro board game CLUEDO
With Additional Material by Mark Bell

ACT ONE

Prologue

(PRE-SET: The great Hall of Boddy Manor is only just visible. Occasionally a lightning flash slightly illuminates an area of the stage via the windows. An old valve radio is USL, its grill light on. Walk in music plays in the auditorium—some old standards from the 1940s linked by an old-style BBC announcer (can include the 'turn off your mobile devices…' announcement with appropriate period jokes, e.g. '…if any of you have brought your transistor radios that is! Ha ha ha'). As the house lights go down the music moves from the house speakers and comes only from the onstage radio. As light come up it changes to . . .)

(Sounds of heavy rain and Rottweiler dogs barking. Dimly lit wall sconces and chandeliers reveal an empty, regal foyer and magnificent front Hall. YVETTE *polishes a glass while listening to the news on an old stand-up radio.)*

NEWSCASTER. *(Old-fashioned plummy BBC voice:)* And now the news: One month after the publication of the Lynskey Tribunal's findings, questions continue to be asked in the House of Commons. The Prime Minister Mr Atlee has assured the house that immediate steps will be taken:

(A startling crash of thunder/lightning illuminates the glass-paneled front door, revealing the silhouette of a man holding an umbrella.)

CLEMENT ATLEE'S VOICE. This will not stand. This will not go unpunished. Junior Minister Mr John Belcher and Bank of England director Mr George Gibson have resigned from their posts with immediate effect. And as for Mr Sidney Stanley, if that indeed is his real name, let me say this; He should quit Britain! And furthermore, anyone else with secrets to hide should be looking over their shoulder!

(The front door creaks open, unheard by YVETTE. *Enter* WADSWORTH, *the butler, dressed perfectly, shaking off and stowing his umbrella and hat, a twinkle in his eye.)*

NEWSCASTER. *(Beneath the following dialogue until cut off:)* In other happier news, for the first time since the war, suits, costumes and overcoats are off ration! So it's time to get out there and costume up ladies! Gentlemen, time for a visit to Savile Row perhaps! And now everyone can wrap up warm in a nice new coat! Which brings us to the weather. Storms continue to batter the south of England, bringing danger of flooding and dangerous driving conditions in many areas. Surprisingly the North East of England is basking in the mildest February weather ever recorded! With the small town of Shiney Row in Northumberland setting an all-time record. Now back to the light program.

(Music resumes. WADSWORTH *moves behind* YVETTE.*)*

WADSWORTH. *(Rather intimately:)* Yvette?

*(*YVETTE *yelps, startled!)*

YVETTE. Bleedin' eck. *(Then, off* WADSWORTH's *look:)* Ooo la la monsieur! I didn't hear you come in! You frightened me half to death!

WADSWORTH. Wouldn't want to do that. There are so many better ways to die. *(Then:)* Please turn off that noise.

*(*YVETTE *turns off the radio – cutting off the news/music.)*

WADSWORTH. Is everything ready?

YVETTE. Oui.

WADSWORTH. Good. *(Calling off:)* Cook?

(In a flash of thunder/lightning, a formidable COOK, *dressed perfectly, appears from the Kitchen.)*

COOK. You called, sir?

WADSWORTH. Everything on schedule?

COOK. Dinner will be ready at 7:30. *(Revealing a butcher knife on a music sting:)* Sharp.

(Just then, the doorbell rings. They look out.)

WADSWORTH. Ah. Right on time. You have your instructions?

COOK. Yes.

YVETTE. Yes. Oui.

WADSWORTH. Very well then.

(He moves to the door. YVETTE *exits with the radio.* COOK *exits to the Kitchen.)*

WADSWORTH. *(Just before opening the door:)* Let the game begin.

Scene 1

(The Hall/The Lounge.)

(Dogs bark. Rain storms.)

*(*WADSWORTH *straightens his jacket, smooths his hair, looks at his pocket watch and grandly opens the front door. Note: These actions repeat with increasing speed each time Wadsworth opens the door.)*

*(*COLONEL MUSTARD, *officious, stands in the doorway, shielding himself from the rain. He wears a decorated Colonel's uniform.)*

*(*COOK *reenters during the following to assist with coats and such.)*

WADSWORTH. Good evening.

MUSTARD. *(Entering fully:)* Good evening. I'm not sure if I'm in the right—

WADSWORTH. Yes, indeed you are expected, Colonel.

MUSTARD. How do you— *(know who I am?)*

WADSWORTH. *(Interrupting:)* It is Colonel Mustard, is it not?

MUSTARD. No, that's not my name. My name is Colonel—

WADSWORTH. I believe it's been recommended that tonight you use a pseudonym.

MUSTARD. Oh, no thank you. I took an antihistamine before I set off.

WADSWORTH. *(Taking his coat:)* May I take your coat?

MUSTARD. Oh. All right. I suppose I . . .

*(*YVETTE, *at the bar cart, now pops open a bottle of champagne, à la gunshot, startling* MUSTARD, *who yelps.)*

WADSWORTH. Not to worry, Colonel. It's just the maid, in the Hall, with the champagne cork.

YVETTE. *(Offering:)* Champagne?

MUSTARD. *(Taking the glass, flummoxed by her beauty:)* Oh, uh, don't mind if I . . .

YVETTE. *(Interrupting:)* Zis way monsieur.

MUSTARD. *(Following her anywhere:)* Ah. Thank you.

> *(YVETTE escorts MUSTARD to the door of the Lounge. The doorbell interrupts. They look out.)*

MUSTARD. Are you expecting someone else?

WADSWORTH. Indeed. I'll be with you in a moment.

YVETTE. Through there, Colonel.

MUSTARD. With pleasure, my dear.

> *(YVETTE opens the Lounge door, escorting MUSTARD inside.)*
>
> *(WADSWORTH, jacket, hair, watch – opens the front door.)*
>
> *(Rain storms. MRS WHITE stands, tragic and morbid, dressed in funeral clothing, guarding herself from the rain. Over her face is a mesh black veil.)*

WADSWORTH. Do come in, madam. You are expected.

> *(She enters more fully, WADSWORTH at her heels.)*

WADSWORTH. Welcome.

WHITE. *(With a confident mystique:)* Do you know who I am?

> *(She pulls back her veil to reveal her face.)*

WADSWORTH. Only that you are a socialite to be known this evening as Mrs White.

> *(She slips off her cloak, black with a brilliant white inside.)*

WHITE. Yes.

> *(WADSWORTH catches it gracefully.)*

WHITE. It said so in my letter. But, why—?

WADSWORTH. *(Interrupting:)* May I introduce you? Mrs White, this is the maid, Yvette.

> *(Music sting. The women notice each other and flinch.)*

WADSWORTH. I see you two know each other.

WHITE. *(Deliberately lying:)* We've never met.

YVETTE. *(Cheekily:)* Champagne?

WHITE. *(Pointedly:)* I think not.

WADSWORTH. Please, warm yourself in the Lounge.

WHITE. Why, do I look cold?

WADSWORTH. A bit. *(Shepherding her into the Lounge—then:)* I'll be right with you.

(WADSWORTH now pulls the Lounge wall open slightly, making the interior of the Lounge partially visible as WHITE steps through the door, noticing MUSTARD.)

WHITE. Oh. Hello.

MUSTARD. Hello. Pleased to meet you.

WHITE. I'm rarely pleased to meet anyone.

(Doorbell rings. They look out.)

WHITE. More?

WADSWORTH. Oh, yes.

(WADSWORTH shuts the Lounge door.)

(Rain storms. YVETTE opens the front door to a music sting. MRS PEACOCK, middle-aged, wealthy, and batty, stands, shielding herself from the rain with a box of chocolates.)

YVETTE. Bonjour madame. Please, come in from the rain.

(As PEACOCK enters . . .)

WADSWORTH. Mrs Peacock, I presume.

PEACOCK. Who? *(Realizing:)* Oh yes! That's me!

WADSWORTH. Cook, will you please take Mrs Peacock's stole.

(With a music sting, the women recognise each other. They flinch!)

WADSWORTH. I see you two are acquainted.

PEACOCK. *(Discarding her stole into the COOK's arms:)* Don't be ridiculous, I've never seen this woman before in my life.

YVETTE. *(Offering:)* Champagne?

PEACOCK. My lips belong to the Lord!

WADSWORTH. Please, make yourself comfortable in the Lounge.

PEACOCK. Thank you.

(As WADSWORTH escorts her to the Lounge, she remembers the lavishly wrapped box of chocolates in her hands.)

PEACOCK. Oh! For your hospitality . . . *(An aside:)* And there's a . . . 'gift' under the caramels for you, butler.

WADSWORTH. How . . . sticky.

PEACOCK. I expect to be treated like the wife of a . . .

(The doorbell rings. They look out.)

WADSWORTH. Do hold that thought. Right this way. After you, Mrs Peacock.

(He opens the door to the Lounge.)

PEACOCK. *(Enamored by the doorframe:)* Oh my, look at the detail of this moulding; this is quite a magnificent mansion, isn't it . . .

(She screams, startled to find WHITE and MUSTARD.)

PEACOCK. Who are you?!

WHITE. Welcome to the party.

MUSTARD. *(Tickled pink:)* This is turning out to be quite the crowd.

(As YVETTE closes the Lounge door, dogs bark. Rain storms. WADSWORTH opens the front door.)

(REV. GREEN, straight as an arrow, stands in a trench coat, holding an umbrella. He does not enter, but remains in the doorway, anxious.)

GREEN. Is this the right address to meet a . . . Mr Boddy?

(The dogs bark wildly.)

WADSWORTH. *(To dogs:)* Sit!

(GREEN frantically sits. Dogs stop barking.)

WADSWORTH. No. Not you, sir.

(GREEN stands sheepishly.)

GREEN. Sorry, sorry.

WADSWORTH. Please, come in.

GREEN. *(Entering more fully:)* Excuse me, I suppose this letter has me rather anxious.

WADSWORTH. You must be Reverend Green.

GREEN. *(Painfully lying:)* Yes. That's exactly who I am.

WADSWORTH. Welcome, sir.

(GREEN hands his umbrella to YVETTE as he steps into the Hall.)

GREEN. *(Noticing the interior:)* Oh my! This isn't at all what I expected.

WADSWORTH. I find if you expect nothing, you're never disappointed.

GREEN. *(Not to be misunderstood:)* Oh, I'm not disappointed . . .

(The doorbell rings, interrupting. They look out.)

WADSWORTH. Pardon me, sir.

(WADSWORTH *opens the door [music sting] to find* PROFESSOR PLUM *[smoking a pipe] with* MISS SCARLETT *[smoking a long, thin cigarette] standing behind him.)*

WADSWORTH. Good evening.

PLUM. *(Reading authoritatively from his letter in the doorway:)* 'Please arrive at 7:30 sharp on Saturday evening.' *(A glance to his watch:)* Well, here I am . . .

WADSWORTH. Professor Plum.

PLUM. If you say so.

SCARLETT. *(Stepping in more fully:)* Well, well, well. And I thought I'd seen everything . . .

WADSWORTH. Miss Scarlett. Welcome. I didn't realise you and the Professor were acquainted.

SCARLETT. We're not.

(SCARLETT *continues as* PLUM *gives his coat to* COOK.)

SCARLETT. The bridge is washed out from the rain. My car broke down, and this Professor offered to give me a ride.

PLUM. *(Smarmily to* GREEN:*)* I'm hoping she'll return the favour one day.

SCARLETT. You couldn't afford it. *(Back to* WADSWORTH.*)* I didn't realise we were headed to the same place until . . . we arrived.

(*Dialogue continues as* SCARLETT *gives her coat to* COOK. GREEN *also tries to hand his coat to* COOK. *He tries to hang it somewhere and she eventually, reluctantly takes it.)*

WADSWORTH. *(To* PLUM:*)* How was your drive?

PLUM. It's a long haul.

WADSWORTH. Indeed, it is a long hall. But then, it's a very large house. *(Then:)* This way please.

(WADSWORTH *points the way to the Lounge.* SCARLETT *absorbs the grandeur of the manor.)*

SCARLETT. Heavens . . . what is this ghastly old place anyway?

WADSWORTH. This old place? Oh, this . . . is Boddy Manor.

(Thunder/lightning. They jump. GREEN *more so than the others.)*

WADSWORTH. Cook. Dinner?

COOK. Directly.

(COOK moves to the Kitchen.)

WADSWORTH. *(Showing SCARLETT, PLUM, and GREEN to the Lounge:)* Appetisers in the Lounge. After you.

(WADSWORTH opens the Lounge fully to reveal the interior.)

PLUM. Hors d'oeuvres. Good, I'm starving.

GREEN. Funny. I haven't much of an appetite at all.

SCARLETT. *(Entering the Lounge and noticing the others)*: I say, this really is a party.

PLUM. *(As he enters the Lounge:)* Well, greetings all. It's a pleasure for you to meet me. *(Noticing drinks, he helps himself.)* Oooh, cocktail hour!

GREEN. *(As he enters the Lounge:)* There are so many of you—I didn't realise . . .

WADSWORTH. *(Interrupting:)* Right. Good then. You're all here.

(Then, swiftly paced:)

WADSWORTH. Colonel Mustard.

MUSTARD. Present.

WADSWORTH. Miss Scarlett.

SCARLETT. Hmm.

WADSWORTH. Mrs White.

WHITE. Yes.

WADSWORTH. Professor Plum.

PLUM. Right.

WADSWORTH. Reverend Green.

GREEN. That's me.

WADSWORTH. Mrs Peacock.

PEACOCK. *(With a rather formal, yet floppy curtsey:)* How d'you do?

WADSWORTH. Greetings. I am Wadsworth, the butler. *(Then:)* Tonight, as you may have surmised, nobody is being addressed by their real name. A courtesy your host has provided to ensure your privacy. I suggest you follow his lead and refrain from revealing too much about yourselves this evening. You never know when—

(COOK *strikes a gong, interrupting. They jump!* GREEN *spills champagne all over himself.*)

WADSWORTH. *(Calmly, as always:)* Ah. Dinner.

GREEN. *(Wiping himself up:)* Oh, sorry. Sorry. I'm a bit clumsy, I suppose.

PLUM. Dinner? That was more like a cocktail minute.

SCARLETT. Mr Wadsworth, you were saying . . . 'You never know when' . . . what?

WADSWORTH. What?

SCARLETT. What?

WADSWORTH. Hm? *(Then – showing the way:)* This way please.

(YVETTE *has handed* GREEN *a fresh glass of champagne just in time for* COOK *[who has reentered] to hit the gong again. They jump!* GREEN *spills his drink again.*)

WADSWORTH. We really oughtn't keep her waiting. Cook can get tetchy. Ladies and gentlemen, follow me. The Dining Room is right this way.

(*Transition music. The cast follows* WADSWORTH *from the Lounge to the Dining Room. Behind them, as the Lounge closes,* YVETTE *and* COOK *each push on the Dining Room table. Chandeliers fly in.*)

Scene 2

(*The Dining Room.*)

(*The* GUESTS *arrive to find a beautifully set table with seven places. There are no chairs. The* GUESTS *stand around the table looking lost.*)

COOK. *(Yelling at them:)* Well get a chair then!

(*Chairs are brought from various parts of the Hall in a hasty, scared way. Lights change to only light the Dining Room downstage.*)

WADSWORTH. You'll find your names beside your places.

ALL. *(Ad-libbing:)* Do you see my tag? / Is that me? / Is that you? / Oh, here you are, Reverend Green. / This looks lovely. *(Etc.)*

(*They take their places,* MUSTARD *next to* SCARLETT *next to* GREEN *next to* PEACOCK *next to* WHITE *next to* PLUM.)

WADSWORTH. Please be seated.

MUSTARD. *(Not yet seated:)* This place—at the head of the table—is that for you?

WADSWORTH. Indeed no, sir. I don't sit. I am merely a humble butler.

MUSTARD. What exactly do you do?

WADSWORTH. I buttle, sir.

COOK. *(Presenting the meal grandly:)* Dinner is served.

WADSWORTH. Thank you, Cook.

> *(As the* GUESTS *settle in their seats,* YVETTE *and* COOK *serve them soup.)*
>
> *(*PEACOCK *taps her knife against her glass to get the* GUESTS' *attention. [The waving of her knife is a bit threatening to* GREEN *beside her.])*

PEACOCK. *(Tucking a napkin in at her neck à la a bib:)* All right then, what's all this about, butler; this dinner party?

WADSWORTH. 'Ours not to reason why,
Ours but to do and die . . . '

GREEN. *(Anxiously:)* Die?

WADSWORTH. Merely quoting, sir, from Alfred, Lord Tennyson.

SCARLETT. I prefer Kipling myself. *(Offering a basket of dinner rolls to* MUSTARD:*)* Do you like Kipling, Colonel?

MUSTARD. *(Helping himself:)* Oh yes, I'll eat anything. *(Then:)* So, who is our host? Is this where he sits?

WADSWORTH. *(Pouring wine:)* All in good time, sir.

> *(As* YVETTE *serves soup to* PEACOCK—*)*

PEACOCK. What is that smell? It's something . . . familiar.

YVETTE. Soupe d'ailerons de requin. Shark's fin soup.

PEACOCK. *(Gleefully:)* My favourite!

COOK. *(Deliberately:)* I know.

> *(*COOK/PEACOCK *exchange a sinister glance.)*

YVETTE. Bon appetit!

> *(*YVETTE *and* COOK *exit. The* GUESTS *sip their soup.* PEACOCK *slurps.)*

PEACOCK. *(Slurping slightly—muttering:)* This is delicious. *(Slurping louder now—under her breath:)* Oooh, this is yum yum yummy yum yum yum.

> *(PEACOCK, ever enjoying her soup, continues her slurping. The other* GUESTS *begin making sounds of their own: the tapping of a plate, the scuff of a chair, the clink of a wine glass, the opening and closing of a lighter. Perhaps we hear the click click click of* YVETTE's *heels as she comes out to fill wine glasses. We may even hear a cat sound. The sounds build in intensity as they begin to sound quite rhythmic and musical.)*

> *(After reaching a cacophony,* WADSWORTH *enters and strikes the gong. The* COOK *and* YVETTE *enter with silver trays of food—six plates of drab-looking meat and two veg.)*

COOK. Meat!

> *(The* COOK *reveals the food to a cat's meow.)*

COOK. Who's going to be next!

YVETTE/COOK. Who!

> *(She slams down the plates in rhythm, moving from stage right to stage left. When she has placed all the plates, she turns and walks back stage right, the silver tray hitting the heads of all six* GUESTS—*also in rhythm.)*

> *(*WADSWORTH, YVETTE, *and the* COOK *exit. Slowly. Music. The* GUESTS *eat and drink. At certain moments throughout, each guest picks up an item from the table, lights shift and the guest strikes a threatening pose. The remaining guests react in horror. For example,* WHITE *picks up a butter knife and holds it above her head before she butters a roll.* MUSTARD *struggles to open a jar, but it looks like he is strangling someone.* YVETTE *enters with a large pepper shaker and it looks like she might strike* PEACOCK *with it.* PEACOCK *screams!)*

> *(*GREEN *begins to choke on a piece of food. The guests one by one stare at him in horror, perhaps it is a real murder! Finally,* SCARLETT, *realizing what is really happening, slaps him hard on the back and the morsel of food pops out of* GREEN's *mouth and into his—or someone else's—glass)*

> *(The* GUESTS *all sit in silence, fearful and suspicious. After a moment of uncomfortable silence,* PEACOCK *can stand it no longer . . .)*

PEACOCK. Well, I guess I'll break the ice, I mean, I'll be the one to get the ball rolling, I mean, I'm used to being a hostess; it's an integral part of my life as the wife of a . . . *(Declining wine with a gesture, carrying on talking without pause:)* Oh, I forgot we're not supposed to say who we really are. But, oh well, I mean, I have no idea what we're doing here, but I'm very intrigued and oh, my, that soup was delicious wasn't it?

(The GUESTS *stare at her, bewildered.)*

GREEN. I know who you are.

PEACOCK. You do?

GREEN. I work in Westminster.

PLUM. Westminster? *(To* PEACOCK*:)* So you must be a politician's wife, Mrs Peacock?

PEACOCK. *(With renewed confidence:)* Yes, I am.

SCARLETT. *(Cheekily:)* Who's your husband? Perhaps I know him.

PEACOCK. I . . . well, he's . . . *(Deflecting:)* Mrs White, you've been awfully quiet. What does your husband do?

WHITE. Nothing.

PLUM. Nothing?

WHITE. Well, he . . . just lies around on his back all day.

PEACOCK. How lazy!

SCARLETT. Not necessarily.

(Thunder/lightning. GREEN *spills his drink all over* SCARLETT's *chest.)*

GREEN. *(Mopping up* SCARLETT's *chest with his napkin:)* Sorry, sorry—I'm afraid I'm a little accident-prone.

SCARLETT. *(Relishing his discomfort:)* That will be five pounds please Reverend.

GREEN. *(Awkwardly mortified:)* I beg your pardon?!

PEACOCK. *(Tapping him on the shoulder:)* Reverend Green—what do you do in Westminster?

GREEN. Oh, I'd rather not say. I like to follow the rules.

PEACOCK. *(Frustrated:)* Well, if I wasn't trying to keep the conversation going, then we would just be sitting here in an embarrassed silence.

PLUM. Are you afraid of silence, Mrs Peacock?

PEACOCK. *(Anxiously:)* Yes. No. Why?

PLUM. In my professional opinion, it seems you suffer from what we call 'pressure of speech.'

MUSTARD. Is that an official diagnosis?

WHITE. Are you a doctor, Professor?

PLUM. In psychological medicine.

WHITE. Do you practise?

PLUM. *(Laced with shame:)* Not anymore. *(Then:)* I currently work for the government.

WHITE. Ah, another politician.

PLUM. Not exactly. I do research for U-NO WHO.

WHITE. *(Genuine:)* Who?

PLUM. *(Pleased with how clever he is:)* U-NO WHO!!!

> *(The other guests get involved, trying to guess who, never letting* PLUM *explain, until . . .)*

PLUM. No!!! Actually it's . . . A branch of the—

WHITE. The Department of Education—

PLUM. No no no no . . .

GREEN. The Northumberland Rotary Club—

PLUM. No—

SCARLETT. The French—

MUSTARD. That new National Health Service—

PLUM. No no no—oh will you just listen will you! As a matter of fact, it's a branch of the United Nations Organization: The World Health Organization.

WHITE. Ahh. 'U-NO WHO.' *(Explaining to the table to show she got it first:)* It's an acronym.

MUSTARD. *(From the other side of the table—densely:)* I have a sister who was a gymnast.

PLUM. *(Flummoxed by* MUSTARD:*)* You are a *real* colonel, aren't you?

MUSTARD. *(Officiously:)* I am, sir.

SCARLETT. Aren't you going to mention the coincidence that you also live in Westminster, Colonel?

MUSTARD. How did you know that?

SCARLETT. *(With a twinkle:)* Oh, I've seen you before.

GREEN. So, Miss Scarlett, does this mean that you live in Westminster too?

SCARLETT. *(With a sly smile:)* Soho actually, but close enough.

PEACOCK. Does anyone here not live in Westminster? Or Soho?

(They ALL look at each other, putting together the coincidence.)

PLUM. *(Fearfully:)* Oh. Then, is this about the Lynskey business?

GREEN. I'm not a black marketeer! I am not involved with vile corruption!! I'm a Conservative.

(Thunder.)

(MUSTARD stands, fed up.)

MUSTARD. Wadsworth, we've had about enough of this! Where's our host, and why have we been brought here?!

(The doorbell rings. They look out.)

WADSWORTH. Ah, speak of the devil. Pardon me, please.

(WADSWORTH exits through the door.)

SCARLETT. I've got an idea.

(Quickly SCARLETT grabs her empty water glass and runs to the door. She places her ear against her glass against the door.)

(Throughout the following dialogue, they all follow suit, lining up, single file, behind SCARLETT, ears to glasses to ears of the GUEST in front of them, as though they are able to hear through the glass, through the ear of the GUEST, through the door. They talk on top of each other . . .)

WHITE. Oh yes, good thinking, Miss Scarlett.

PEACOCK. What are we doing?

PLUM. The acoustic coupling between the door and the glass allows sound waves to travel from one side to the other.

(Once the rest are in position, poor MUSTARD, confused, simply stands outside the group, and raises his glass to his own ear.)

(We hear WADSWORTH's muffled voice from the Hall.)

WADSWORTH. All the guests have arrived as expected, sir. *(Then:)* Everything's going according to plan. *(Then:)* We will meet you in the Study.

(MUSTARD gently taps his glass like a microphone ['is this thing on'] to try to get it to work.)

(A fraction of a moment passes and WADSWORTH *reenters the Dining Room from a door on the other side of the room. He clears his throat, startling the chain of* GUESTS, *causing a kerfuffle. They startle, surprised at his entrance, and try to cover their faux pas.)*

ALL. *(Ad-lib:)* Lovely door. / Oh, hello Wadsworth, we were just playing a game. / Well, look who's back. / We didn't hear a thing. / There's a door over there?! *(Etc.)*

PEACOCK. *(Fed up, removing the napkin from her dress and slamming the table:)* Oh, for God's sake! Who was at the door?! I demand to know what's going on!

WADSWORTH. *(Evermore the butler:)* Can I interest any of you in fruit or dessert?

ALL. No!

WADSWORTH. In that case, may I suggest that we adjourn to the Study for coffee and brandy, at which point I believe your newly arrived host will reveal his intentions, your letters will be explained and . . . the game will be afoot.

> *(Thunder/lightning! As they move to the Study, transition music plays and the* GUESTS *start to move. Then the music stops suddenly as . . .)*

COOK. Well take your chairs!!!

> *(She mutters things about 'people never know anything' and 'do I have to manufacture everything,' etc, as* YVETTE *and* COOK *pull the table offstage and* WADSWORTH *opens the Study door, letting the* GUESTS *in. Then opens the Study wall and the set [moved by the cast] spills out to centre stage.)*

Scene 3

> *(The Study.)*
>
> *(*YVETTE *offers drinks from a bar cart.)*

YVETTE. *(Offering:)* Coffee? Brandy? Coffee? Brandy? . . .

WADSWORTH. Thank you, Yvette. That will be all.

YVETTE. Oui, my boosh.

WADSWORTH. Biche.

YVETTE. Biche. Oh sacre bleu.

> *(*YVETTE *exits.)*

GREEN. Well, where is our host?

PEACOCK. He's not here! Nobody's here! What is happening?!

SCARLETT. *(Offering:)* Cigarette? It'll calm your nerves.

PEACOCK. I don't smoke!

> (PEACOCK, *having pulled a flask out of her purse, takes a deep swig.*)

> (During the above, MUSTARD *has found a string and button closure envelope [à la the envelope placed in the centre of the* CLUEDO *board game] on the desk. The envelope reads 'CONFIDENTIAL' in large red letters.*)

MUSTARD. *(Reading:)* 'For Wadsworth. Open After Dinner.' *(Handing it to* WADSWORTH:) It's for you.

> (WADSWORTH *opens and reads it privately.* PLUM *tries to get a glimpse over his shoulder.*)

> (WADSWORTH *blocks his effort. A breath and then . . .*)

WADSWORTH. *(Having finished:)* Right then. Are you comfortable?

MUSTARD. I make a good living.

PLUM. Oh, out with it, Wadsworth!

WADSWORTH. Ladies and gentlemen, these instructions are clear.

SCARLETT. I'm glad something is.

WADSWORTH. It seems the six of you have all received the same letter.

> (*They all reveal their letter on a music sting.*)

> (WADSWORTH *takes the letter from* PLUM *and reads from it.*)

WADSWORTH. 'It will be to your advantage to be present on this date because a Mr Boddy will bring to end a certain long-standing confidential and painful financial liability.'

ALL. *(Ad-libbing:)* Yes! / Yes, that's what my letter said. / Indeed! *(Etc.)*

WADSWORTH. As it turns out, you all have one thing in common.

MUSTARD. That bastard Atlee! We're all being blacklisted ... aren't we?

WADSWORTH. Close, Colonel.

> (*Their proximity is such that* WADSWORTH's *spit has gotten in* MUSTARD's *eye. He wipes it clean.*)

WADSWORTH. You're all being blackmailed.

(Sinister music underscores.)

WADSWORTH. For some considerable time, all of you have been paying more than you can afford to someone who threatens to expose you.

PEACOCK. Oh, please! What's someone going to blackmail me for? I go to church every Sunday!

SCARLETT. Yes my dear, don't we all.

WADSWORTH. Does anyone else wish to deny it?

(They don't.)

WADSWORTH. Until you'd received your letters, you hadn't known who was blackmailing you. But now, I'm sure that even the least discerning amongst you has determined that the man behind your ransom . . . is Mr Boddy himself.

(Music out. They speak at once.)

PEACOCK.	**PLUM.**
Yes, I imagined as much, but who is this fellow?!	And who are you, his 'heavy'? You pompous, sinuous servant!

MUSTARD. It's Mr Boddy? What a scoundrel!!

GREEN.	**WHITE.**
All this stress is not good for my blood pressure!	You think I can't handle a little blackmail?!

SCARLETT. *(Taking the reins:)* Who is this Boddy?!

WADSWORTH. Who Mr Boddy is, is no concern of yours. Suffice it to say, he's a supporter of the current anti-corruption drive, if not of the current 'Labour' Government—

(They ALL laugh.)

WADSWORTH. —and he feels your *activities* have been decidedly, well, corrupt.

(They ALL begin to protest . . .)

WADSWORTH. *(Interrupting:)* My task this evening is to expose your secrets to each other—rendering you all culpable in each other's indiscretions.

PLUM. But we hardly know each other.

WADSWORTH. Precisely.

WHITE. Don't you think that you might spare us this humiliation?

WADSWORTH. I'm afraid I have no choice. We'll start with you, Professor Plum.

SCARLETT. *(Perching on the desk:)* Oooh, this ought to be good.

WADSWORTH. It says here you were once a professor of psychiatry, specializing in pathological, lying lunatics suffering from delusions of grandeur.

PLUM. Yes, but now I work for the government.

WADSWORTH. So, your work has not changed. *(Then:)* But you can't practise medicine anymore, can you? You have been struck off, correct?

SCARLETT. Why? What did he do?

WADSWORTH. You know what male doctors aren't supposed to do with their lady patients?

SCARLETT. Yes?

WADSWORTH. Yes, well, he did.

PEACOCK. *(Harshly whispered:)* You're disgusting.

WADSWORTH. Are you making moral judgements, Mrs Peacock?

PEACOCK. Well, I—

WADSWORTH. *(Interrupting:)* How, then, do you justify taking bribes in return for delivering the Minister, Lord Peacock's votes to certain lobbyists?

PEACOCK. *(Defensive:)* My husband is a paid consultant. There's nothing sinful about that!

WADSWORTH. Not if it's publicly declared. But if you slip cash under the lavatory door at the Savoy? How would you describe that transaction?

SCARLETT. I'd say it stinks.

PEACOCK. *(Accusatorially:)* When were you in that men's room?

PLUM. So, it's true!

PEACOCK. No, it's a vicious lie!

WADSWORTH. But you've been paying blackmail for over a year now to keep that story out of the papers. Seems a little . . . sticky, no?

PEACOCK. Now see here—

WHITE. *(Interrupting:)* Well, I'm willing to believe you. I too am being blackmailed for something I didn't do.

GREEN/MUSTARD. *(Piping up at the same moment:)* So am I.

SCARLETT. Not me.

WADSWORTH. You're not being blackmailed?

SCARLETT. Oh, I'm being blackmailed, all right. But I did what I'm being blackmailed for.

PLUM. What did you do?

SCARLETT. I run my own business.

WHITE. That's not a crime.

SCARLETT. You didn't ask what kind of a business I run.

PLUM. All right, what kind of business do you run?

SCARLETT. I provide gentlemen with the company of a young lady.

PEACOCK. *(Outraged:)* An escort service?! In Soho?!

WHITE. How scurrilous.

MUSTARD. I'm sure some people are just a little lonely.

PLUM. *(Scoffing:)* A man who needs to pay to spend time with a woman. *(He laughs . . . 'That's a problem* I'll *never have.')*

> *(He sheepishly takes a business card* SCARLETT *has pulled out and tucks it in his coat pocket.)*

PLUM. Thank you.

GREEN. Is that how you knew Colonel Mustard works in Westminster? Is he one of your clients?

MUSTARD. Certainly not!

GREEN. I was asking Miss SCARLETT.

MUSTARD. *(To* SCARLETT:*)* Well, you tell him it's not true!

SCARLETT. 'It's not true.'

PLUM. Is that true?

SCARLETT. No, it's not true.

GREEN. Ha-hah! So it is true!

WADSWORTH. A double negative!

MUSTARD. Double 'negative'? You mean you have—photographs?

WADSWORTH. That sounds like a confession to me. In fact, the double negative has led to proof positive. I'm afraid you gave yourself away.

MUSTARD. Are you trying to make me look stupid in front of the other guests?

WADSWORTH. You don't need any help from me, sir.

(MUSTARD *starts to register the insult—but . . .*)

WADSWORTH. Colonel, it appears that you hold a sensitive security post in the War Office. Those 'negatives' would most certainly compromise your position.

PLUM. *(With a wink:)* And what position exactly were you caught in, Colonel?

MUSTARD. This is an outrage!

WADSWORTH. *(Changing focus:)* Let's see, who's next?

(*He charges towards* GREEN *but spins on a dime at the last moment to . . .*)

WADSWORTH. Mrs White, you've been paying our friend the blackmailer ever since your husband died under, shall we say, mysterious circumstances.

WHITE. Say what you want. I didn't kill him.

MUSTARD. Then why are you paying the blackmailer?

WHITE. I don't want another scandal, do I?

PLUM. Another?

WHITE. We had a very humiliating confrontation. He had threatened to kill me in public.

SCARLETT. Why would he want to kill you in public?

WADSWORTH. I think she meant that he had threatened, in public, to kill her.

(*They all react with understanding.*)

WHITE. It was all over the papers.

WADSWORTH. And yet he was the one who died. Not you, Mrs White, not you.

WHITE. He was found dead at home. Unclothed. His head had been cut off and so had his . . . you know.

(*She gestures in the direction of her groin. They all react.*)

WHITE. But, I didn't do it. I'd been out all evening, at the movies.

SCARLETT. What was showing?

WHITE. *The Naked Alibi.*

SCARLETT. A likely story.

WADSWORTH. But he was your second husband. Your first also disappeared.

WHITE. That was his job—he was an illusionist.

WADSWORTH. But he never reappeared.

WHITE. He wasn't a very good illusionist.

WADSWORTH. *(Now to* GREEN:*)* And lastly, Reverend Green, who is a . . .

GREEN. I don't need you to unmask me, Wadsworth. I know what you're going to say about me!

WADSWORTH. What's that?

GREEN. 'Reverend Green, who is a homosexual.'

MUSTARD. Not me.

GREEN. I beg your pardon?

MUSTARD. You asked, 'Who is a homosexual,' and I said, not me.

*(*GREEN *and* WADSWORTH *share a baffled moment.)*

WADSWORTH. Yes, thank you, Colonel. *(To* GREEN:*)* But, there's more to it than that, Reverend Green.

GREEN. How do you mean?

WADSWORTH. There's evidence to support the question of . . . your politics.

GREEN. My politics?! Since when is supporting the Conservative party a crime?

WADSWORTH. You are a signed-up member of the Conservative Party, a 'True-Blue' Tory through and through, but you neglected to vote for MR CHURCHILL in the last election!!!

(Gasps from EVERYONE.*)*

WADSWORTH. That's grounds for an ousting if ever there was one.

GREEN. But voting records are confidential!

PEACOCK. Everything has its price, Reverend Green.

WADSWORTH. So—there you have it.

ALL. *(Bordering hysteria:)* Have what?!

WADSWORTH. A crooked Minister's wife, a lascivious doctor, a disloyal Tory, and so forth . . . not exactly adhering to the standards of behaviour that made the British Empire great, are you?

SCARLETT. *(Knowingly:)* Depends on who you ask.

PLUM. But if this Boddy chap is such a noble civilian himself, then why didn't he report us to the authorities?

WADSWORTH. And give up the opportunity to turn a profit? Come now, Professor. What could be more Old Empire than that?

MUSTARD. *(In earnest:)* Kedgeree.

(Collective bemusement.)

SCARLETT. All right, Wadsworth—so we're being blackmailed by a renegade Imperialist. Where does that leave us?

WHITE. Where is this Mr Boddy?

MUSTARD. And what does he want from us?

PEACOCK. Who cares?! I'm not waiting to find out! I've done nothing wrong! I'm leaving!

(She charges to the door.)

WADSWORTH. *(Blocking her efforts:)* I'm sorry, Mrs Peacock. You can stay in denial, but you cannot leave this house!

PEACOCK. I am the wife of a Minister, a member of the House of Lords! You can't tell me what to do!

(She tries to open the door.)

PEACOCK. Locked?!

(Sinister music underscores.)

WADSWORTH. Indeed. All the doors are locked. The windows are barred. And the grounds are patrolled by vicious dogs.

(Dogs bark.)

WADSWORTH. There's no way out!

(Lightning. They ALL *begin screaming at* WADSWORTH.*)*

ALL. Locked?! / This is an outrage! / You can't hold us hostage! / Why?! *(Etc.)*

WADSWORTH. *(Gaining their attention:)* Ladies and gentlemen, allow me to introduce your host for the evening, and your blackmailer for life . . .

(Lightning.)

WADSWORTH. Mr Boddy.

(Music sting as BODDY *appears in the Study doorway with confident charm. Music out.)*

BODDY. How d'you do?

(They speak at once.)

PEACOCK.
Who do you think you are?
I'll have you brought before
the House of Lords!

PLUM.
I thought aristocrats were
supposed to be good-looking,
you swine!

GREEN.
I say, would I like to give you a
biff on the nose! And I don't
even like confrontation!

SCARLETT.
Why are you blackmailing us?
I'm frustrated that I find
you attractive!

MUSTARD.
Bribing all these good people?
I don't get it! What's in it for you?!

WHITE.
You're such a typical man!
Better off dead!

*(*WHITE *emerges at the front of the group to expertly knee* BODDY *in the groin.)*

SCARLETT. *(Impressed:)* Ooooh. Mrs White, in the Study with her knee!

WHITE. Thank you. I've studied martial arts.

(They take a wary step away from WHITE.*)*

WADSWORTH. *(Getting their attention once more:)* There is one more piece of information you may like to have.

ALL. What?!

WADSWORTH. The police will be here in less than an hour!

ALL. What? / Why? / The police?! / What are you talking about? *(Etc.)*

BODDY. *(Recovering:)* Unless . . .

ALL. Unless, what?

*(*BODDY *refers to his briefcase.)*

BODDY. You agree to 'double down.' *(After a beat.)* As the Americans say.

SCARLETT. And why would we agree to that?

BODDY. Because if you don't, I'll put this briefcase—containing all the evidence needed to expose your wrongdoings—in the hands of the police, the press, and the Lynskey Tribunal. With the right spin, those coves can make a traitor out of anyone. And I rather think some of you would face a lifetime of prison, and others, a lifetime of ghastly shame.

ALL. That's why you've brought us all here?! / You devil! / Get that briefcase! / You're taking advantage of a tenuous political situation! *(Etc.)*

BODDY. Unless . . .

ALL. *(Including* WADSWORTH*:)* Unless what?!

BODDY. Well, there is something you could do for me that would change the game. Something I just can't bear to do myself.

ALL. *(Including* WADSWORTH*:)* What?!

BODDY. *(To* GUESTS*:)* Have a seat, please. Take a pew.

> *(The* GUESTS *move to the chairs. The ladies sit, the gentlemen stand behind. After a brief silence . . .)*

GREEN. *(Re: the desk:)* Is it all right if I just stand here . . .

> *(Before he can get the word out,* GREEN *knocks an object off the desk and dives down to catch it before it smashes.)*

GREEN. *(Bouncing back up:)* Sorry, sorry. Little accident-prone. Sorry.

> *(*BODDY *exits.)*

GREEN. What's he doing?

WADSWORTH. I really don't know. *(Then — genuine to* BODDY*:)* What's this about, sir?

BODDY. *(Entering:)* In this box, there are six packages that I thought our guests might find useful this evening.

> *(*BODDY *begins to empty a box full of packages [each the colour of one of the guests' names] into the arms of* WADSWORTH*.)*

WADSWORTH. Packages?

BODDY. Presents, if you will. I'm a generous sort of fellow.

WADSWORTH. Are you?

BODDY. Wadsworth, will you please see to it that each guest receives a gift?

WADSWORTH. Gladly.

> *(*WADSWORTH *moves to distribute the gifts.)*

BODDY. *(Pouring himself a brandy:)* Anyone care to make a guess as to what's in your boxes?

SCARLETT. Perfume?

WHITE. Turkish delight?

PEACOCK. A rare single-malt Scotch whiskey?

BODDY. *(With a laugh:)* Aren't guessing games fun? *(Then:)* Please—do open them.

> (SCARLETT *opens her box. Puzzled, she lifts out a heavy brass Candlestick.*)
>
> (*Music sting. She looks at* BODDY.)

SCARLETT. A Candlestick? What's this for?

> (*One by one, with a music sting, each of the* GUESTS *open their boxes, pulling out their 'gift.'*)

MUSTARD. A Spanner . . .

GREEN. A Lead Pipe . . .

PEACOCK. A Dagger . . .

PLUM. A Revolver . . .

WHITE. Ahhhhhh! A snake! Oh, no. It's a Rope.

> (*Then:*)

BODDY. In your hands you each have a lethal weapon.

> (*They gasp.*)

BODDY. You all came tonight because you believed the evidence against you was so terrible that you would do anything to keep it a secret. I'm putting that theory to the test.

WADSWORTH. You are?

BODDY. Our Wadsworth here is the only other person who knows your secrets; and it's costing us all dearly to keep him quiet.

GREEN. What do you mean?

BODDY. I wouldn't have to double your payments if I didn't have to pay Wadsworth for his silence.

ALL. Wadsworth?!

WADSWORTH. That's a lie!

BODDY. He may look suave and charming . . .

WADSWORTH. True.

BODDY. But really, he's conniving and manipulative.

WADSWORTH. False!

BODDY. Why do you think he's called the police?

PLUM. *(To WADSWORTH:)* You called the police?

WADSWORTH. Only because HE instructed me to do so!

BODDY. Did I? *(Then:)* Ladies and gentlemen . . . if you can manage to get rid of Mr Wadsworth, I'll have no need to increase your blackmail or expose you to the police.

PLUM. Get rid of?

PEACOCK. *(To WHITE:)* Does he mean . . . kill him?!

BODDY. In fact, if you can eliminate Wadsworth . . .

WHITE. Yes, I think that's what he means.

BODDY. Who not only knows all of your secrets, but also mine—then I will eliminate your blackmail altogether and be done with this terrible business once and for all.

WADSWORTH. You would never!

PLUM. But why make us do it, Boddy?! Why don't you do your dirty work yourself?

GREEN. Indeed!

BODDY. Why should I when the six of you are so uniquely motivated and armed?

SCARLETT. What a true gentleman.

WADSWORTH. After all I've done for you?! *(To GUESTS:)* He's a liar! I'm one of you! I'm not a butler! I'm an indentured servant!

BODDY. A familiar refrain. *(Darkly:)* Don't make a scene, Wadsworth. It's over. *(To GUESTS:)* The police are on their way. Now's your chance. The only way for you to end your blackmail and avoid finding yourselves on the front pages is for one of you to kill Wadsworth NOW!

(He switches off the lights. BLACKNESS. CHAOS. SCREAMS. A GUNSHOT. MORE CHAOS AND SCREAMS. Lights.)

(BODDY sits by the desk. Slumped. Head down. EVERYONE else is spread throughout the Study.)

WHITE. It's Mr Boddy!

WADSWORTH. *(Enormously relieved:)* Oh thank God.

SCARLETT. Is he breathing?!

(They rush to him in a hubbub.)

PLUM. *(Cutting off the chatter:)* Stand back, I'm a doctor!

(They move back. PLUM *gives* BODDY *a cursory examination.)*

PLUM. He's dead.

WHITE. Who had the gun?

PLUM. I did.

PEACOCK. So you shot him!

PLUM. I didn't!

PEACOCK. If you didn't, who did?

PLUM. Somebody grabbed it from my hand, and the next thing I knew there was a shot!

*(*WADSWORTH *turns* BODDY *over.)*

WADSWORTH. There's no gunshot wound.

WHITE. He's right. There isn't.

SCARLETT. *(Re: a hole in the wall:)* Look, there's a bullet lodged in the wall!

MUSTARD. Eagle eye, Miss Scarlett.

GREEN. Well, if the bullet's over there, then how did he die over here?

PLUM. I don't know! I'm not a forensics expert.

SCARLETT. Something else must have killed him.

WHITE. One of us must have killed him.

(They all look at each other—and their weapons—nervously aware that a murderer is present amongst them.)

GREEN. Well, don't look at me! I didn't do it!

ALL. *(Joining in:)* Me neither! / I didn't do it! / What're you looking at me for?! *(Etc.)*

*(*PEACOCK, *unable to find a drink elsewhere, goes to* BODDY's *body, who is still holding a goblet.)*

PEACOCK. I need a drink!

(She pries the goblet from BODDY's *dead hand, raises it to her lips . . . She downs it just as . . .)*

PLUM. Maybe Mr Boddy was poisoned by the brandy!

*(*PEACOCK *spits out the brandy—all over* PLUM *and dead* BODDY.*)*

PEACOCK. *(Screaming:)* Poison!?!

(PEACOCK continues to scream. GREEN tries to comfort her . . .)

GREEN. There, there, Mrs Peacock—

(She still screams.)

GREEN. I'm sure you'll be just fine—

(She still screams.)

GREEN. There's nothing to—

(WHITE takes over, pushing GREEN out of the way. She slaps PEACOCK, who falls onto the chairs, silenced, as the GUESTS gasp.)

SCARLETT. *(Offering an excuse:)* Thank God, someone had to shut her up.

PLUM. *(To GREEN:)* Was the brandy poisoned?

GREEN. How should I know?

SCARLETT. Looks like now we'll never know.

GREEN. Unless she dies too.

(They all hurry over and stare at PEACOCK. Suddenly YVETTE SCREAMS from another part of the house. They all look out, terror on their faces.)

(Transition music.)

WADSWORTH. The screams are coming from the Billiard Room!

(The GUESTS rush around. GREEN has the Lead Pipe in his hand. The Study is taken off by the cast as they move to outside the Billiard Room.)

Scene 4

(The Hall outside the Billiard Room)

(YVETTE's screams are louder now as WADSWORTH and the GUESTS [except PEACOCK] arrive at the door of the Billiard Room. WADSWORTH tries the handle. The door is locked.)

WADSWORTH. It's locked! *(Into the door:)* Who's in there? Who's screaming?

YVETTE. *(From inside:)* C'est moi!

WADSWORTH. Yvette?!

YVETTE. Oui!

WADSWORTH. *(Into the door:)* Yvette, are you all right?!

YVETTE. *(From inside:)* No!

MUSTARD. Yvette?! Are you alive?!

(YVETTE opens the door, revealing herself, in a puddle of tears, fuming!)

YVETTE. Of course I'm alive, you bleedin' idiot. *(French again:)* Ee-diot! *(Turning to* WADSWORTH*:)* No zanks to you—Wadsworth! You've locked us up in zis house wiz a murderer!

WHITE. So the murderer is here?

YVETTE. Oui!

GREEN. Where?

YVETTE. Where? Here! We're all looking at him.

(PEACOCK enters, out of breath.)

YVETTE. Or her . . .

MUSTARD. What took you so long?

PEACOCK. *(Winded and hysterical:)* I'm an old woman who may or may not have been poisoned! It's amazing I'm anywhere!

YVETTE. *(Back to her point:)* I heard you all in ze Study—one of you is ze killer!

PLUM. How could you hear us in 'ze' Study?

YVETTE. I was listening! I have a tape recorder in ze Billiard Room connected to ze Study! Monsieur Boddy asked me to record your converzation!

PLUM. Why would he ask you to do that?!

YVETTE. For more evidence, of course! Wadsworth revealed your secrets in ze Study; now zey are all recorded.

PLUM. What a snake! I've got to destroy them! Where are the tapes?

YVETTE. Who cares about ze tapes?! What about ze body?!

MUSTARD. What body?

ALL. Boddy's body!

MUSTARD. Right you are.

WHITE. But, Yvette, why were you screaming in there, all by yourself?

YVETTE. Because I was frightened! I also drank ze Cognac. Maybe I am poisoned too! *(And more to the point:)* Plus, one of you is ze killer! Monsieur Boddy is dead!

GREEN. *(To* YVETTE:*)* We have to figure out which one of them did it!

PEACOCK. What do you mean 'which one of them'?

GREEN. Well, I didn't do it!

WADSWORTH. Well, one of you did. I would have killed him myself, but I didn't have access to a weapon.

SCARLETT. Don't look at me! All I got was a Candlestick!

PLUM. Maybe it wasn't one of us!

GREEN. Who else could it have been?

WHITE. Who else is in the house?

YVETTE. Only ze Cook.

ALL. *(Looking out:)* ZE COOK!

> *(Transition music as* WADSWORTH *leads the* GUESTS *to the Kitchen.)*

MUSTARD. Weapons ready chaps.

WHITE. She could be hiding anywhere.

PLUM. Look everywhere.

GREEN. I hope there's no blood.

YVETTE. Sacre bleu!

SCARLETT. Where is she?

PEACOCK. Oh God!

Scene 5

> *(The Kitchen.)*
>
> *(They enter the Kitchen. There is a large pantry.* GREEN *no longer has the Lead Pipe. They look for* COOK.*)*

PLUM. As far as I can tell, the Cook's not here.

PEACOCK. What a lovely Kitchen. My husband and I had a kitchen very similar to this in our first London townhouse. It has such a homey feel, doesn't it . . .

(As she reminisces, GREEN *trips, accidentally causing the large pantry to open. The* COOK's *body, Dagger in her back, tumbles out onto a quite unsuspecting* GREEN.)

*(*PEACOCK *SCREAMS.)*

WHITE. It's the Cook!

SCARLETT. With a Dagger in her back!

MUSTARD. Someone must've killed her!

PLUM. Yes. She's dead.

GREEN. *(Descending to the floor under* COOK's *weight:)* I didn't do it!

*(*GREEN *lands on the ground beneath the* COOK. *Nobody moves.)*

WADSWORTH. This makes two.

PLUM. Two what?

WADSWORTH. Murders.

PEACOCK. *(Hysterical:)* I hate murders!

MUSTARD. I think you'd better explain yourself, Wadsworth.

WADSWORTH. Me?

MUSTARD. Well, who else would want to kill the Cook?

SCARLETT. *(A little laugh:)* Dinner wasn't that bad.

MUSTARD. How can you make jokes at a time like this?

SCARLETT. It's my defence mechanism.

MUSTARD. Some defence! If I were the killer I'd kill you next.

*(*EVERYONE *gasps!)*

MUSTARD. I said 'if.' There's only one admitted killer here, and it's not me. *(Pointing to* WHITE:*)* It's Mrs White!

*(*EVERYONE *gasps!)*

WHITE. I've admitted nothing.

MUSTARD. You paid the blackmail. How many husbands have you had?

WHITE. Mine or other women's?

MUSTARD. Yours.

WHITE. Five.

MUSTARD. Five?

WHITE. Yes, just the five. Husbands should be like Kleenex—soft, strong and disposable.

MUSTARD. Well, if it wasn't you, who was it? Who had the Dagger?

PLUM. It was Mrs Peacock!

> (EVERYONE *gasps!*)

PEACOCK. Yes. But I put it down.

MUSTARD. Where?

PEACOCK. In the Study. Any one of us could have picked it up.

ALL. Well, I didn't. / It wasn't me. / I never even saw the Dagger. *(Etc.)*

PEACOCK. Well then, it must have been . . . Reverend Green!

GREEN. *(Under the* COOK's *body—muffled:)* Can somebody please help me?!

> *(They look, gasping!)*

WADSWORTH. Good Lord, let him up!

PLUM. *(Moving to assist:)* You really have to learn to speak up for yourself, Reverend Green.

> (MUSTARD *and* PLUM *lift the* COOK's *body off of* GREEN. GREEN, *gasping, recovers, getting up.*)

GREEN. *(Breathless:)* Oh my God. Oh my God.

> (WADSWORTH *steps over* GREEN, *who crawls away [and will ultimately take a swig from Peacock's flask], as dialogue continues.*)

WADSWORTH. Gentlemen, might I suggest we take the Cook's body into the Study.

> (WADSWORTH *hoists the* COOK *out of* MUSTARD *and* PLUM's *arms and onto his back.*)

SCARLETT. Why?

WADSWORTH. For starters, when the police arrive, if they find this . . .

> *(He dumps the* COOK's *body off his back and into the arms of the rest of the group.)*

WADSWORTH. We'll all be in custody and under suspicion for murder.

PEACOCK. Murder!

WADSWORTH. And secondly, I'm the butler. I like to keep the Kitchen tidy.

(They heave-ho, grumbling as they do, puppeteering the COOK's *body from the Kitchen back to the Study to transition music.)*

Scene 6

(The Study.)

*(*WHITE *carries the* COOK *on her back.)*

SCARLETT. *(To* WHITE:*)* That's it. That's it. *(To* GREEN/MUSTARD/PLUM:*)* Gentlemen?

GREEN/MUSTARD/PLUM. Oh yes. / Sorry. / Yes, quite right. / Of course. / You take that leg. / On three. / Three! / Put her down for goodness sake. / What about on the chairs? / Where will we sit? *(Etc.)*

(To the tail end of transition music, the GUESTS, *except* WADSWORTH, *enter the Study. They stop and slowly look back to the chair where* BODDY *was. HE'S GONE!)*

PLUM. The body's gone!

(They freeze! They drop COOK *to the ground with a THUD! Just then,* WADSWORTH *enters, breathless.)*

WADSWORTH. What are you all staring at?

PLUM. Nobody.

WADSWORTH. What do you mean?

PEACOCK. *(Panic-stricken:)* Nobody. No body. Mr Boddy's body. It's gone!

WHITE. Maybe he wasn't really dead.

PLUM. He was!

WHITE. We should have made sure.

PLUM. I thought I had!

MUSTARD. So was he dead or wasn't he?!

GREEN. Perhaps he *was* dead, but someone moved him!

SCARLETT. Who would move him?

WHITE. And why?!

GREEN. How should I know?!

PLUM. Well, if he's not here—then where is he?

PEACOCK. Oh my. All this excitement. If you'll excuse me, I have to uh . . . is there a little girl's room?

YVETTE. Oui oui, madame.

PEACOCK. No, I just want to powder my nose.

(They both look out.)

YVETTE. Zere's a toilette outside ze Billiard Room.

(PEACOCK exits.)

WADSWORTH. *(Clocking* PEACOCK's *exit:)* Uhhhh . . . *(Then:)* I don't mean to alarm anybody, but we do currently have the small issue of two dead bodies: one missing, one present—and the imminent arrival of the police . . .

SCARLETT. The bridge is washed out; that should buy us some extra time.

YVETTE. But I don't want extra time! I want ze polize to arrive! I am trapped in zis houze wiz a murderer!

PLUM. But once the police get here, the rest of us are doomed.

MUSTARD. *(Taking charge:)* Wadsworth, am I right in thinking that there is nobody else in this house?

WADSWORTH. Um, no.

MUSTARD. Then there is someone else in this house?

WADSWORTH. Sorry, I said 'no' meaning 'yes.'

MUSTARD. 'No,' meaning 'yes'?

WADSWORTH. Yes.

MUSTARD. Look, I want a straight answer.

(They look at him.)

MUSTARD. Wadsworth—is there someone else in this house, yes or no?

(WADSWORTH considers this carefully.)

WADSWORTH. Um . . . No.

MUSTARD. No, there is? Or no, there isn't?

WADSWORTH. Yes.

MUSTARD. There seems to be some confusion about whether or not we are the only people in this house.

WADSWORTH. There isn't.

MUSTARD. There isn't any confusion or there isn't anybody else?

WADSWORTH. Either. Both.

MUSTARD. Just give me a clear answer.

WADSWORTH. What was the question?

MUSTARD. Is there anyone else in the house?

ALL. No!

MUSTARD. That's what he says, but does he know?!

SCARLETT. Look, we've got a killer on the loose, the missing dead body of Mr Boddy, a Cook with a Dagger in her back, and all these easily accessible weapons—the Rope, the Revolver, the Candlestick, the Spanner—and . . . where's the Lead Pipe?

> (PEACOCK *screams. She enters, stumbling into the room with* BODDY *hanging all over her. It looks like* BODDY *is attacking her.*)

PLUM. It's Mr Boddy!

GREEN. He's attacking her.

> (*While* PEACOCK *continues her hysteria, the bloodied* BODDY *falls off her and onto the ground. The Lead Pipe protrudes from his skull.*)

GREEN. (*Grossed out:*) Oh God, he's so bloody!

PLUM. Stand back! (*Completing a second cursory exam:*) He's dead.

SCARLETT. That's what you said the last time.

PLUM. I believe in second chances.

WADSWORTH. Mr Boddy? Dead? Again?

PEACOCK. I'm going to faint!

WADSWORTH. I'll catch you!

> (PEACOCK *collapses in* WADSWORTH's *arms. He releases her and she falls back with a thud.*)

WADSWORTH. Sorry.

WHITE. Mrs Peacock? Mrs Peacock? Mrs Peacock? Mrs Peacock? Mrs Peacock? Mrs Peacock? (*Etc.*)

PEACOCK. (*Woozy from the floor:*) Yes?

WHITE. Where did this happen?

PEACOCK. In the bathroom! I opened the door and there he was! At first, I thought he was attacking me, but then I realised he'd been left propped up against the doorframe, dead, just waiting to fall on someone!

(She pulls a tiny bottle of booze out from her cleavage and downs it.)

WHITE. Who would do such a thing?

PLUM. It takes a lot of courage to kill someone twice.

SCARLETT. It's what we call overkill.

GREEN. But why?!

PLUM. What's the difference?

SCARLETT. Makes a difference to him!

WADSWORTH. *(Losing it:)* Makes a difference to us! We've got to find out who killed him, where and with what!

PLUM. *(Referencing the Lead Pipe in* BODDY's *head:)* Seems like it was probably the Lead Pipe.

WADSWORTH. Ten points, Professor Plum.

MUSTARD. What kind of game are you playing, Wadsworth?

WADSWORTH. This isn't a game!

PLUM. *(To* GREEN:*)* You! The Lead Pipe belonged to you!

GREEN. But I dropped it while running to the Kitchen!

PLUM. People don't just drop murder weapons!

GREEN. I didn't know it was a murder weapon when I dropped it!

WHITE. So anyone could have picked it up?

WADSWORTH. *(Becoming unhinged:)* Yes of course, but who did?!? Who did pick up the Lead Pipe? Who picked up the Lead Pipe and brutally murdered Mr Boddy, leaving him dead and bloodied in the bathroom? Who did that? Who?! Who?!?! Who?!?!?!

SCARLETT. *(From the desk:)* Calm down butler! While you lose your marbles, I'm over here trying to do something useful! Have you all forgotten about the evidence against us?

ALL. The evidence!

(They move towards SCARLETT, *who opens the briefcase.)*

SCARLETT. It's empty!

(They gasp!)

WADSWORTH. Empty?!

MUSTARD. Then where's all the evidence?

WADSWORTH. I told you Boddy was a liar! Had the evidence in his briefcase, my foot!

GREEN. We must find that evidence!

SCARLETT. And destroy it!

MUSTARD. *(Becoming officious:)* Evidence against us aside, first things first. We're in a room with two dead bodies.

YVETTE. And ze cops are on zeir way!

MUSTARD. Let's move the corpses to those seats so they look less dead.

> *(They do. What follows is a farcical moving of the two dead bodies from the floor onto the chairs.)*

PLUM. *(Stepping over* COOK *to get to* BODDY:*)* Some party this is turning out to be.

YVETTE. *(Crossing to the* COOK:*)* Help me, Monsieur Green.

GREEN. *(Dubious:)* Reverend. Well, all right.

> *(YVETTE/GREEN drag COOK, while PLUM drags BODDY.)*

WADSWORTH. Careful. Don't get offal on the ground.

MUSTARD. *(Impressed by* PLUM *dragging* BODDY's *body:)* Solid battlefield technique, Professor Plum. Never leave a man behind.

WHITE. Cadavers are heavier than they seem, aren't they?

WADSWORTH. I wouldn't know.

WHITE. Quite. Me neither.

GREEN. *(Lifting* BODDY *up:)* Upsy-daisy.

WHITE. *(Then re: the* COOK:*)* Here, prop her up.

PEACOCK. *(From her unhelpful perch on the desk:)* Aren't you all strong and virile?

> *(She drinks from a flask.)*
>
> *(Throughout the hubbub, the GUESTS ad-lib appropriately until the bodies are both in position on the chairs with GREEN pinned between them. GREEN, gagging, un-pins himself, escaping the horror. The GUESTS prop both bodies [Dagger and Lead Pipe fully visible] upright.)*

WHITE. Good. They just look asleep.

SCARLETT. Forget about the bodies! We need to do something about this room full of murder weapons and the homicidal maniac on the loose!

WADSWORTH. Let's put the weapons in the box!

(WADSWORTH starts to put the remaining weapons in Boddy's box.)

SCARLETT. What good will that do?

WADSWORTH. Then we'll close the lid.

WHITE. Most murderers know how lids work, Mr Wadsworth.

WADSWORTH. I know! We'll put the box in the safe!

SCARLETT. *(Looking all around:)* Terrific! Where's the safe?

WADSWORTH. In the Hall!

(Transition music. They move to the Hall.)

WADSWORTH. Shush.

(They stop. Listen. More transition music as they move again.)

Scene 7

(The Hall.)

(They arrive and WADSWORTH tinkers with the bottom of a large framed portrait hanging between two doors.)

SCARLETT. I don't see a safe.

PLUM. *(Re: the art:)* Is that an original Hogarth, Mr Wadsworth?

WHITE. Those are quite valuable.

PEACOCK. Now is not the time for art appreciation! Butler . . .

(Before PEACOCK can finish her thought, WADSWORTH opens the painting on the wall to reveal a safe.)

GUESTS. *(Gently impressed:)* Ohhh.

(As WADSWORTH throws the box in and locks the 'painting' . . .)

MUSTARD. A hidden safe behind a portrait. How original!

WADSWORTH. There! Locked!

YVETTE. Voila!

MUSTARD. What are you going to do with the key to the safe, Wadsworth?

YVETTE. Oh yes! Ze key!

WADSWORTH. I'll put it in my pocket.

PEACOCK. But what if you're the murderer?

WADSWORTH. I'm not.

PEACOCK. But what if you are?

WADSWORTH. I've an idea—we'll throw it outside.

YVETTE. Oui! À l'extérieur!

PEACOCK. But it's raining 'à l'extérieur!'

WADSWORTH. I'm not suggesting we go outside. I'm suggesting we stay inside but throw away the key.

PLUM. *(Warily:)* But you'd have to open the door, wouldn't you?

WADSWORTH. I would.

PLUM. But what if the killer is outside?

GREEN. Better out than in!

PLUM. Yes! We'd want to keep him outside, wouldn't we? If we open the door we risk letting him back in.

WHITE. But maybe, if we open the door, we'd encourage the killer to go out!

SCARLETT. The killer seems to be doing a fine job of opening and closing doors all by himself. I don't see how us opening the door for one tiny second could possibly make any sort of a difference.

MUSTARD. But what if we open the door, throw away the key, and the killer catches it. Then the killer would have the key we're trying to confiscate!

WADSWORTH. We might be overthinking this. *(Then:)* I'm going to throw away the key. Follow me.

(Transition music as the GUESTS *run towards the front door.)*

Scene 8

(The Front Door.)

*(*WADSWORTH *leads* YVETTE *and the* GUESTS *towards the front door. He opens the door to throw away the safe key, but*

shockingly, a MOTORIST *stands at the door, poised to knock. The* GUESTS *scream.)*

WADSWORTH. *(Screaming:)* Not now!

(WADSWORTH *slams the door in the* MOTORIST's *face. The* GUESTS *are breathless with fear.)*

GREEN. Was that the killer?!

WHITE. He didn't look like a killer.

PLUM. *(A dig:)* Takes one to know one.

MUSTARD. Leave him to me. Interrogation is my speciality.

*(*MUSTARD *opens the door.)*

MUSTARD. How do you do?

MOTORIST. I'm sorry . . . *(As he enters, searching for words:)* I didn't mean to disturb the whole household, but my car broke down out here, and I was wondering if I could use your phone.

MUSTARD. *(Accusatorially:)* Are you a killer?

MOTORIST. What? No!

MUSTARD. *(Entirely convinced:)* All right. *(Showing him in:)* This way please.

(As the others start to protest . . .)

MOTORIST. Thank you.

(He steps fully into the mansion.)

MOTORIST. Well? Where is it?

MUSTARD. What? The body?

(The others gasp!)

MOTORIST. *(Realizing:)* The phone. What body?

WADSWORTH. What? There's no body. There's nobody.

MUSTARD. Yeeees. There's nobody in the Study.

(MUSTARD *has inadvertently pointed to the Study. The* MOTORIST *starts walking towards it.* EVERYONE *realises that's where the bodies are!)*

ALL. *(Preventing him from going to the Study:)* No!!!

WADSWORTH. No, no that phone's been disconnected. But I think there's one in the Lounge.

MOTORIST. Righty-ho.

(WADSWORTH brings the MOTORIST to the door of the Lounge as the others look on.)

WADSWORTH. Directly through this door.

MOTORIST. Thank you.

(WADSWORTH opens the door, lets the MOTORIST in, closes and locks the door.)

WADSWORTH. *(To GUESTS with renewed intense urgency:)* Now listen . . . we haven't much time. Our task is twofold. ONE: Find the evidence! TWO: Find the murderer!

PLUM. We've got one potential suspect contained in the Lounge—but that leaves the whole rest of this place up for grabs. Who knows what's behind all these doors.

MUSTARD. I suggest we handle this in proper military fashion. We split up and search the house.

PEACOCK. Split up!?

MUSTARD. Yes! We'll split up into pairs. That way none of us will be alone.

PLUM. But if we split up into pairs, whichever one of us is paired with the killer might get killed!

YVETTE. Mon Dieu!

MUSTARD. But then we would have discovered who the murderer is!

PEACOCK. But the other half of the pair would be dead!

MUSTARD. This is war, Peacock! Casualties are inevitable. You cannot make an omelette without breaking eggs—every cook will tell you that.

PEACOCK. But look what happened to the Cook!

GREEN. Colonel, are you willing to take that chance?

MUSTARD. What choice do we have?

SCARLETT. None.

GREEN. I suppose you're right.

MUSTARD. *(Officious:)* All right, troops. Divide and conquer. I'll split us into pairs. Eenie-meenie-miney . . .

WADSWORTH. *(Per the rhyme:)* No. *(Then taking the reins:)* Mrs White, you come with me. Professor Plum, you're with Mrs Peacock. Yvette, you go with Reverend Green; and Miss Scarlett, you're with Eenie Meenie.

PEACOCK. But what if someone doesn't come back?

WADSWORTH. We'll remember you fondly. Now, leave no door unopened. And ... cherish your partner. They might be the last person you ever see.

> *(Music as they* ALL *eye each other suspiciously in a cinematic pose. Productions may add in some direct address from* WADSWORTH *to introduce the ...)*

WADSWORTH. Ladies and gentlemen. The bar is now open and mine's a sherry.

Interval

ACT TWO

Scene 9

(The Hall. They repeat the last lines of Scene 8. WADSWORTH cheers his glass of sherry to the audience and takes a sip. He passes the glass to Yvette.)

WADSWORTH. Mrs White, you come with me. Professor Plum, you're with Mrs Peacock. Yvette, you go with Reverend Green; and Miss Scarlett, you're with Eenie Meenie.

PEACOCK. But what if someone doesn't come back?

WADSWORTH. We'll remember you fondly. Now, leave no door unopened. And . . . cherish your partner. They might be the last person you ever see.

> *(Search music: The pairs search the house through an elaborate musical montage of choreographed door slamming and tomfoolery, punctuated by brief vignettes.)*
>
> *(After an initial series of highly stylised crosses and door openings, focus shifts to WHITE and WADSWORTH, now alone in the Hall facing the doors of the Library and Billiard Room on opposite sides of the stage.)*

WHITE. Go on. I'll be right behind you.

WADSWORTH. That's why I'm nervous.

WHITE. But why? It's just us. We're alone.

WADSWORTH. That's just it, Mrs White. No man in his right mind would ever be alone with you.

WHITE. Fine. You go in there and I'll go in here.

(They go to the two upstage doors. They don't go in.)

WHITE. Are you going in?

WADSWORTH. Yes, are you?

WHITE. Yes.

> *(They fake each other out three times in quick succession. Then . . .)*

WADSWORTH. On the count of three. One . . . Three!

> *(A beat and then WADSWORTH and WHITE enter and exit their respective rooms abruptly.)*

WHITE. Nothing in that room.

WADSWORTH. Nothing in that room either.

WHITE. Shall we search the Ballroom?

WADSWORTH. *(Gesturing for her to go first:)* After you.

> *(WHITE and WADSWORTH exit.)*
>
> *(Search music: The other GUESTS crisscross the entry Hall, causing each other to startle.)*
>
> *(MUSTARD and SCARLETT meet in the middle, each holding a notebook and a tiny golf pencil [from the CLUEDO board game].)*
>
> *(They compare their notes and each exit separately as WADSWORTH opens the Library.)*
>
> *(Focus shifts to: PEACOCK and PLUM in the Library.)*

PLUM. *(Seated in an armchair:)* This is quite an impressive Library.

> *(PEACOCK puts a book back in the bookshelf, triggering an elaborate secret panel labelled 'EVIDENCE,' plastered with headshots [in the style of the CLUEDO game cards] and notes detailing the guests' crimes, to flip and appear in the wall directly behind them. They do not see it.)*

PEACOCK. *(Her back now to the secret panel:)* How can I find anything if I don't even know what I'm looking for!

PLUM. *(Reading from a book:)* 'Civilised society is perpetually menaced with disintegration through this primary hostility of men towards one another.'

PEACOCK. Your fancy words don't intimidate me, Professor!

PLUM. I take no credit, Mrs Peacock. *(Re: the book:)* Freud. I think he's onto something.

PEACOCK. Now is not the time for intellectual pursuits! We're supposed to find the evidence!

PLUM. It's a fruitless search, if you ask me. I mean, it's not like we're just going to walk into a room and find the evidence plastered on the wall.

PEACOCK. I suppose you're right.

PLUM. I say, let's go upstairs. Perhaps we'll be excited by something in a bedroom.

PEACOCK. I haven't been excited by something in a bedroom for years.

> *(The Library is closed by WADSWORTH.)*

(The GUESTS *crisscross once more, featuring an unexpected, split-second connection between* YVETTE *and* WADSWORTH.)

(Then, MUSTARD, *solo, crosses the Hall studying an enlarged map of Boddy Manor [which looks identical to the CLUEDO board game].)*

(To the music, each GUEST *round-robins through every door in choreographed mayhem. The group ends with all their heads poking out of one door, which* WADSWORTH *shuts.)*

(The music shifts to sinister as WADSWORTH *opens the Lounge and we find the* MOTORIST *on the phone.)*

MOTORIST. I'm a little nervous. I'm at that big house on the hill, and I've been locked in the Lounge. I didn't expect there'd be a whole group of people here—I think they're having some sort of party; and the funny thing is, I think one of them is my customer.

(As he's talking, the portrait behind him opens and a gloved hand appears behind him with a raised Spanner . . .)

MOTORIST. Yes, my regular Tuesday-night passenger . . .

(The Spanner comes down and into the MOTORIST*'s throat. The murderer's other hand flicks a light switch, turning lights off in the Lounge, which stays open.)*

(Search music continues as the lights shift to find SCARLETT *and* MUSTARD *in the Conservatory, which is opened from the inside.)*

Scene 10

(The Conservatory.)

*(*MUSTARD *searches the Conservatory floor.* SCARLETT *enters slyly, holding Plum's pipe.)*

SCARLETT. *(Whispering conspiratorially:)* Psst!

MUSTARD. Oh, there you are.

SCARLETT. You'll never believe what I found in the hallway. *(Showing:)* Professor Plum's stupid tobacco pipe!

MUSTARD. A-ha! What do you think that means?

SCARLETT. Who knows! But it seems suspicious if you ask me.

MUSTARD. I just did.

SCARLETT. Heavens above, Colonel.

MUSTARD. Well I, I . . . —what room is this anyway?

SCARLETT. Search me.

MUSTARD. *(Frisking her:)* All right.

SCARLETT. Oi! Take your paws off me! It's just an expression!

MUSTARD. My apologies, Miss Scarlett. I struggle with nuance.

SCARLETT. *(Moving on:)* This is the last room left to search in this horrible mansion and we still haven't found the evidence.

MUSTARD. I think this time has been productive nevertheless.

SCARLETT. Aren't you a breath of fresh air.

MUSTARD. You are a brave and determined lady, Miss Scarlett. I've really enjoyed our time together. I hope after this expedition ends we can remain friends.

(SCARLETT continues intensely searching.)

MUSTARD. I mean, really, murders aside, it's just been a lovely group of people all in all. I suppose I would like to hear Mrs White explain when and how she lost her veil in the Billiard Room, but . . .

SCARLETT. *(Grabbing the veil:)* You found White's veil in the Billiard Room? Odd.

MUSTARD. Odd?

SCARLETT. Odd.

MUSTARD. Odd?

SCARLETT. Odd.

MUSTARD. Odd.

SCARLETT. Odd.

MUSTARD. Odd.

SCARLETT. Odd.

MUSTARD/SCARLETT. Odd.

(MUSTARD accidentally leans on the wall sconce, which moves like a lever.)

(A trap door opens.)

SCARLETT. *(Gasp:)* A trap door! *(Then:)* A trap door leading to a secret passage! Come on!

MUSTARD. *(Clearing his throat:)* Uh . . . Ladies first, Miss Scarlett.

SCARLETT. *(Rolling her eyes:)* How heroic.

(SCARLETT pushes MUSTARD into the passage. The next section starts with MUSTARD half in the Lounge and half in the Conservatory. MUSTARD exits again.)

MUSTARD. It's scary.

SCARLETT. Get in there.

MUSTARD. All right. All right.

(MUSTARD heads into the passage, followed by SCARLETT.)

Scene 11

(The Lounge.)

(A secret panel opens and [AUXILIARY] SCARLETT and MUSTARD climb out of it as the dialogue continues. The room is dark. The dead MOTORIST in the chair is unnoticed . . . for now.)

(Please note: SCARLETT and MUSTARD are substituted by an auxiliary man and woman, dressed as Scarlett and Mustard. The lighting is such that we can't see their faces and the real Scarlett and Mustard continue their dialogue from offstage or via pre-recorded voiceover.)

MUSTARD. Where are we now?

SCARLETT. How should I know? The lights are off.

MUSTARD. Well turn them on!

SCARLETT. I would if I could see anything!

MUSTARD. Well I'm going to feel my way around.

SCARLETT. Don't get any funny ideas.

MUSTARD. *(Feeling:)* A table . . .

SCARLETT. *(Feeling:)* A telephone . . .

MUSTARD. A chair . . .

SCARLETT. A body . . .

(SCARLETT and MUSTARD stop dead in their tracks.)

SCARLETT/MUSTARD. A body!!! Ahhhhhh!!!!!!!!!!!!!!!

SCARLETT. Find the door!

MUSTARD. Get me out of here!

(They find the door but the door is locked.)

SCARLETT/MUSTARD. HELP! HELP! MURDER! MURDER!

(The stage is now divided in two, with inside the Lounge being stage left, and outside the Lounge being stage right.)

(The GUESTS scurry towards the Lounge from all over the house, ad-libbing, as they make their way to the door—realizing the door is locked . . . As WADSWORTH approaches the Lounge door, he closes the Lounge back up, so only the Hall is visible. At the same time YVETTE closes the Conservatory.)

ALL GUESTS. LET US IN! LET US IN!

SCARLETT/MUSTARD. *(Voices:)* LET US OUT! LET US OUT!

WADSWORTH. We can't let you out! The door to the Lounge is locked!

SCARLETT. *(Through the door:)* You had the key, Wadsworth! You locked the Motorist in here!

WADSWORTH. That's right! I did! I do! *(He checks his pockets:)* I don't! The keys are gone!

ALL. Gone?!

YVETTE. I have an idea!

(YVETTE runs to the safe/portrait.)

SCARLETT. *(Through the door:)* There's a murderer on the loose! Please get us out of here!

(PLUM walks back from the door, at his most macho.)

PLUM. There's no alternative. I'm just going to have to break down the door. *(To the others:)* Stand back! I'm a doctor!

(Just as he backs up to prepare to run, YVETTE comes back from the safe holding the gun.)

YVETTE. Stand back! I'm a woman. A French woman!

(PLUM backs into YVETTE. Their crash causes her gun to go off, firing upwards. The chandelier above—in slo-mo—falls, pinning GREEN beneath it as the GUESTS react [also in slo-mo]!)

GREEN. *(In slo-mo via V.O.:)* Can somebody please help me?

(We restore to regular speed. All the GUESTS scream as GREEN rolls out from beneath the chandelier which nearly crushed him!)

(Note: If you do not have a flying chandelier for this section, the chandelier may be 'mimed' falling by the cast, who then produce a real chandelier at the end and land this on Green, still in slo-mo. Or, Green may dodge the chandelier at the last moment and move

upstage, only to be hit by a piece of falling ceiling plaster [thrown from offstage].)

SCARLETT/MUSTARD. *(Through the door:)* What happened?! What was that?! Help! Murder! Help! *(Etc.)*

YVETTE. I will help you!

(YVETTE, still determined to save the day, points the gun to the Lounge door. With surprising expertise, she fires the gun twice at the lock.)

YVETTE. I'm done shooting at you! Ze door is open! You can come out now!

(The real MUSTARD and SCARLETT exit the Lounge.)

MUSTARD. *(Angrily, to YVETTE:)* Why were you shooting at us?

YVETTE. To open ze door!

MUSTARD. But you could have killed us!

YVETTE. *(Defensively:)* I said 'stand back'!

MUSTARD. *(To WADSWORTH:)* Let's add 'finding the key to the Lounge' to our priority list.

PLUM. Say, Frenchy—where did you get that gun anyway?

YVETTE. Ze zafe. It was unlocked!

ALL. Unlocked!?!?

WADSWORTH. Impossible! I have the key! *(He checks his pocket.)* No I haven't! It's gone!

ALL. Gone?!

MUSTARD. Not to flog a dead horse, but, again, I feel like having all the keys is really— *(important.)*

PLUM. *(Interrupting:)* I thought you said you'd throw away the key to the safe, Wadsworth!

WADSWORTH. I did say that! But I didn't do that! We got distracted by the Motorist at the door and I forgot. One of you must have snatched the keys from my pocket when we were searching the house.

PLUM. So whoever took the keys, is the killer.

WADSWORTH. Precisely.

SCARLETT. Speaking of the killer, you know there's a dead body in the Lounge? That Motorist is dead!

(She opens the Lounge door. They all peek in.)

PEACOCK. Which one of you killed him?

SCARLETT. *(Outraged:)* We found him, together!

MUSTARD. And he was already dead! With a Spanner shoved down his throat.

GREEN. But the door to the Lounge was locked!

SCARLETT. We went through a secret passage we found in the Conservatory.

PLUM. A secret passage?! Who designed this place?

WADSWORTH. John Waddington . . . Ltd.

(The doorbell rings. They look out. They stand still, frozen in terror. They wait. And hope. Doorbell again. They look to the front door. Doorbell rings a third time. They huddle, worrying aloud.)

(KNOCK KNOCK KNOCK.)

WADSWORTH. Don't worry, it's not the police.

BOBBY. It's the police!

(EVERYONE gasps!)

ALL. *(Ad-libbing:)* What should we do? / Let's hide! / Shhh! / You're being too loud! / Maybe this time it's the killer! *(Etc.)*

PLUM. *(Within the melee, taking the gun from YVETTE and stashing it on his body:)* Quick! I'll hide the gun!

GREEN. I'm going to open the door.

ALL. No!

GREEN. It's the decent thing to do.

(He's run up to the front door, the GUESTS at his heels.)

BOBBY. Open the door!

(GREEN opens the front door. A BOBBY stands there.)

BOBBY. Good evening, sir.

GREEN. Good evening, Officer. We've been expecting you.

BOBBY. You have?

GREEN. We haven't?

BOBBY. I got a tip about an abandoned car near the gates of this house. Did a motorist stop by for help, by any chance?

(They try to smooth away his suspicions.)

ALL. No.

GREEN. *(On the heels of 'No':)* Yes.

BOBBY. *(Sceptically:)* There seems to be some disagreement. Any road up, can I come in and use the telephone?

ALL. No!

GREEN. Of course you may, Officer. There's a telephone in the Lounge.

(SCARLETT, *who is closest to the Lounge door, blocks it.*)

SCARLETT. Out of order.

GREEN. Of course. My mistake. You can use the phone in the Study.

(PLUM, *who is closest to the Study door, blocks it.*)

PLUM. Occupied.

GREEN. Ahhhh . . .

WADSWORTH. *(Taking over:)* If you please, sir, you may use the phone in the Library. Right this way.

BOBBY. You're all acting rather peculiar.

WADSWORTH. It's because our chandelier fell down.

ALL. Yes. / Exactly. / That's true. / We loved that chandelier. *(Etc.)*

WADSWORTH. It could have killed us. But don't worry, the maid will clean it up.

BOBBY. That's all well and good, but . . . what's going on in the Lounge and Study?

WADSWORTH. Lounging. Studying. This way . . .

BOBBY. Let me have a look.

WADSWORTH. No thank you.

BOBBY. What?

WADSWORTH. *(Deflective:)* Hm? *(Then:)* This way, please.

BOBBY. Actually, I'd like to take a look around if you don't mind.

WADSWORTH. Of course, Officer. *(Forcibly walking him downstage—slowly:)* Follow me. I'll take you on a grand tour of Boddy Manor.

(*Simultaneously, the* GUESTS *huddle up, quietly whispering together to come up with a plan, while* YVETTE *gets rid of the chandelier.*)

WADSWORTH. This home was built by Lord Reginald Boddy in 1784 . . .

SCARLETT. We've got to cover our tracks and get rid of this Bobby!

WADSWORTH. This way please. *(Distracting him:)* Lord Boddy had been declared Lord Boddy after somebody discovered an antibody that would save everybody.

> (WHITE, PEACOCK, MUSTARD *and* YVETTE *head to the Study where* BODDY *and* COOK's *bodies remain.)*

> (PLUM, SCARLETT, *and* GREEN *head to the Lounge where the* MOTORIST's *body remains.)*

WADSWORTH. *(Desperately trying to distract—he drops to the floor—nearly singing/doing snow angels:)* Notice the mahogany floor. *(Then—vibrantly:)* Did you know, in the 17th century, the buccaneer Anne Bonny recorded the use of mahogany for making canoes? *(He mimes rowing a canoe:)* Can you canoe?

BOBBY. *(Baffled:)* What?

> *(The two groups have each entered their respective rooms. The* BOBBY *turns around to find the stage bare.)*

BOBBY. Oi—where'd everybody go?

WADSWORTH. *(Continuing his desperate tour:)* Notice the brass doorknobs. Crafted specifically for Lord Boddy by his buddy in 1878—

BOBBY. *(Irritated:)* I don't care about the doorknobs, sir! What's going on around here? What are you hiding in those two rooms?!

WADSWORTH. *(Trying to cover:)* Uh . . . which two rooms?

BOBBY. The Lounge and the Study!

WADSWORTH. Oh . . . Oh. Ohhhhh. Those two rooms—

BOBBY. Yes!

> (BOBBY *approaches the Study door.* WADSWORTH *blocks his path.)*

WADSWORTH. No! Officer, I don't think you should go in there.

BOBBY. Why not?

WADSWORTH. Because it's . . . all too shocking!

> (BOBBY *shoves* WADSWORTH *aside as the Study opens. As the* BOBBY *enters, the* GUESTS *puppeteer the dead bodies of* BODDY *and* COOK *so they appear to be alive.)*

> *(We hear 1940s jazz on the radio.)*

(YVETTE *dusts the furniture to the beat of the music. She waves flirtatiously at the* BOBBY.)

YVETTE. Hello, Officer! Welcome to ze party!

(WHITE *has set herself up with the dead body of* BODDY *on top of her, to make it appear as if they're making out.*)

(*The* BOBBY *walks past them, embarrassed.*)

BOBBY. Excuse me.

(YVETTE *dusts him.*)

YVETTE. You are excuzed!

(*The* BOBBY *now notices* MUSTARD *seemingly making out with the dead* COOK, *while* PEACOCK, *unseen by the* BOBBY *behind the curtains, uses her hands as if they were the* COOK's *hands, heavily petting* MUSTARD.)

BOBBY. Pardon me.

(*The* BOBBY *moves to exit.* YVETTE *calls after him.*)

YVETTE. Good night, Officer.

BOBBY. Good night!

(SLAM! *The* BOBBY *retreats from the Study back into the main Hall with* WADSWORTH. *As* WADSWORTH *closes the Study, the* GUESTS *react in disgust as they pull away from the dead bodies.*)

BOBBY. That wasn't all that shocking, sir. Those folks were just having a good time— (BOBBY's *moustache falls.*) Took me ages to grow that. Why didn't you tell me this was a party?

WADSWORTH. My . . . apologies Officer.

BOBBY. Well.

WADSWORTH. Well.

BOBBY. I'll just take a peek in the Lounge, if you don't mind.

WADSWORTH. If you insist, Officer.

(BOBBY *has crossed the Hall to the Lounge and opens the door as* WADSWORTH *opens the Lounge wall.*)

(*We hear a different jazz song on a record player.*)

(*The dead* MOTORIST, *an alcohol bottle in hand, appears to be drunk rather than dead. He is propped up in a chair by* GREEN, *who shares the chair with him, also pretending to be drunk.* PLUM *and* SCARLETT *are slow-dancing to the music behind him.*)

BOBBY. *(Speaking into the doorway:)* Pardon me?

GREEN. *(Slurring his words:)* Ev'ning Officer. How do you do? *(To the others:)* It's a nice Bobby!

BOBBY. Are these men drunk?

SCARLETT. Dead drunk. Mr Bobby sir.

PLUM. *(Suddenly sober:)* Boddy!!!!

SCARLETT. *(Explaining:)* Bobby, a nice . . . Bobby!

PLUM. *(Drunk again:)* Ah yes, a police Bobby.

GREEN. *(Offering booze from BODDY's limp hand – splashing booze everywhere:)* Would you like a sip?

BOBBY. Oh, I can't drink while on the job. The Inspector would kill me.

GREEN. Killed if you do, killed if you don't . . .

BOBBY. What?

GREEN. Eh?

PLUM. Have a lovely evening, Officer.

BOBBY. *(With a tip of his hat:)* Same to you.

> *(The BOBBY shuts the door. As WADSWORTH closes the Lounge, SCARLETT and PLUM help GREEN, disgusted, out of the chair.)*

BOBBY. Well . . .

WADSWORTH. *(With slight desperation:)* I can explain everything.

BOBBY. No explanation necessary, sir. There's nothing illegal about any of this.

WADSWORTH. There's not?

BOBBY. Of course not! This is Great Britain—and that was the freedom we fought the war for.

> *(They share a patriotic moment.)*
>
> *(Then:)*

BOBBY. May I use your telephone now?

WADSWORTH. Certainly!

> *(WADSWORTH leads the BOBBY to the Library.)*

WADSWORTH. *(Opening the door:)* The Library, Officer.

BOBBY. Thank you. You can keep my moustache.

(WADSWORTH *closes and locks the door behind him. Then . . .*)

WADSWORTH. *(Nearly whispered:)* All's clear! You can come out now. Well done, all of you. Impressive!

(*All the* GUESTS *emerge into the Hall congratulating themselves.*)

ALL. You really pulled that off. / Nice touch with the alcohol bottle. / I didn't know you had it in you. *(Etc.)*

WADSWORTH. *(Gaining their attention:)* Psst! *(Then:)* All right, I've locked him in the Library . . .

SCARLETT. How'd you do that? I thought you didn't have the keys!

WADSWORTH. I didn't have my right-pocket keys. *(Revealing keys from his other pocket:)* But my left-pocket keys are intact. *(Then:)* Now—let's finish searching the manor! The police are on their way!

PLUM. But, the police already came!

GREEN. Not the 'broken-down car' police, the 'criminal investigation' police.

WADSWORTH. Precisely. *(Then:)* We must find the evidence and we can't afford to have any more murders! This is getting dangerous. Now go!

(*Transition music. The* GUESTS *disperse to search the house! Both the Library and the Billiard Room are opened by cast members on* WADSWORTH's *signal, as if by magic.*)

Scene 12

(*The Library/The Billiard Room*)

(*The* BOBBY *dials the phone. Sinister music underscores.*)

BOBBY. Hello . . . hello . . .

(*The lights go out in both rooms!*)

BOBBY. A power outage?! Must be the storm. *(Then into the phone:)* Oh, hello Inspector? Yes, this is . . . *(Then:)* Hello? Hello? Are you still there? Is this thing working?

(*A dim light now rises on* YVETTE *in the Billiard Room.*)

YVETTE. *(Alarmed by the darkness:)* E-lo? Oo turned out ze lights?! E-lo?!

(*She sees someone in the doorway.*)

YVETTE. Oh! It's only you. You scared me! *(French again:)* I zought you were ze killer!

(Back to the BOBBY.)

BOBBY. Did somebody cut the line? Hello?

(Back to YVETTE . . .)

YVETTE. Oh, did you find a clue? What is zat in your hand?

(A gloved hand holding the Rope emerges from behind YVETTE. A noose flies onto her neck! She struggles in silence.)

BOBBY. *(Into phone:)* Oh, good, you can hear me, sir. You see, I found an abandoned car and wound up in an old mansion, where all the lights just went out. I'm telling you, Inspector, there's something funny going on around here.

(A gloved hand holding a Candlestick emerges from a trap door in the bookshelf.)

BOBBY. They're having some sort of a party and you'll never believe who I just saw . . .

UNSEEN MURDERER. Psst.

BOBBY. Oh 'ello.

(The BOBBY turns around at the sound. The Candlestick descends on the BOBBY. He and YVETTE die at the same moment.)

BOBBY. Oh no.

YVETTE. I'm not really French.

(BLACKOUT.)

Scene 13: The Hall

(The pulsating tone of a telephone off the hook is heard. The Billiard Room and the Library walls are closed in the darkness. A match/candle flickers. In the light of the flame we see WADSWORTH's face. He finds the light panel. Suddenly, the lights turn back on, revealing WADSWORTH fully. The GUESTS pour back onstage.)

ALL. *(Relieved at the lights:)* Ahhh. / Oh, there we are! / Must've been a short in a wire. *(Etc.)*

PEACOCK. Let there be light!

WHITE. *(Quieting everyone:)* Shhh . . .

(Everyone listens.)

WHITE. Do you hear that?

GREEN. Sounds like a telephone is off the hook.

SCARLETT. It's coming from the Library.

PEACOCK. That's where the killer must be!

WADSWORTH. *(Smoothing his hair:)* I'm going in!

SCARLETT. Aren't you afraid?

WADSWORTH. Of course.

PLUM. Of what? A fate worse than death?

WADSWORTH. No . . . just death.

> *(WADSWORTH, followed by the GUESTS, goes to the Library door. He unlocks it. He talks through the door so we cannot see the dead BOBBY.)*

WADSWORTH. He's just sitting there with the phone. And a Candlestick. *(To the offstage BOBBY:)* Excuse me, Mr Policeman. Are you all right? Do you need assistance? A phone book perhaps?

PEACOCK. *(Pushing past WADSWORTH:)* Now listen here copper! The butler asked you a question! Hang up the telephone already, or I will! Do you hear me? Do you hear me?

> *(Nothing happens. PEACOCK kicks her leg through the door and the dead BOBBY falls out of the Library door.)*

> *(PEACOCK SCREAMS! The GUESTS SCREAM!)*

> *(Transition music plays as they run out of the Library.)*

> *(The Library door is closed after the body has been pushed roughly inside as the Billiard Room is opened by the panicking GUESTS.)*

> *(The GUESTS hysterically run until they all arrive and settle in the Billiard Room. Their bodies block the view of the Billiard table.)*

> *(They ALL breathe heavily.)*

WADSWORTH. We should be safe here in the Billiard Room.

> *(They all inhale/exhale. A moment of peace.)*

WHITE. I don't feel safe.

GREEN. I can't relax.

PLUM. How about a game of snooker to pass the time?

ALL. Oh yes. / I love billiards. / Good idea. / Rack 'em up. *(Etc.)*

(They all step aside and reveal YVETTE's *splayed, strangled body hanging off the table!)*

(The GUESTS *scream! Transition music. The Billiard Room is closed by the* GUESTS *as they run to the Hall, continuing to scream, exiting, individually, through all remaining doors. The house is quiet.)*

(Just then . . . the doorbell rings. The front door opens on its own. A cute, perky SINGING TELEGRAM GIRL *tap-dances in the doorframe.)*

YOUNG WOMAN. *(Singing:)* I ... am ... YOUR SINGING TELEGRAM ...

(GUNSHOT! The YOUNG WOMAN *falls dead in the doorway.)*

(Slowly and dejectedly, the GUESTS *come out of all the doors, and notice the sixth dead body in the doorway.)*

Scene 14

(The Conclusion.)

(They collectively take a breath. WADSWORTH, *pushing the* GIRL's *legs out of the way, shuts the front door. They are eerily calm.)*

WADSWORTH. Three murders in three minutes.

MUSTARD. That's a record!

GREEN. Three murders.

PLUM. Six altogether.

SCARLETT. The Cook, Mr Boddy, the Motorist, the Bobby, Yvette, and the Singing Telegram Girl.

PEACOCK. But who is the murderer?!

SCARLETT. That, madam, is the question.

WADSWORTH. Sometimes the most obvious answer is right under our noses. I think the best course of action is to retrace our steps.

(WADSWORTH retraces the entire play, with recreations of benchmark moments and imitations galore, starting at a normal pace and building to a frenzied pace.)

WADSWORTH. It all started like this . . .

(Thunder. Lightning.)

WADSWORTH. At the start of the evening, there was thunder, lightning, the dogs barked.
(Imitating the doorbell:) DING DONG
(As Mustard:) Colonel Mustard.
(Imitating the doorbell:) DING DONG.
(As White:) Mrs White.
(As himself:) Who noticed Yvette.

> *(He replicates the music sting/reactions.)*

(As Peacock:) Mrs Peacock.
(As himself:) Who noticed . . .
(As Cook:) The Cook.

> *(He replicates the music sting/reactions.)*

(As himself:) Then . . .
(As Green:) Reverend Green.

> *(He barks.)*

(As himself:) Sit!

> *(He sits – then stands.)*

(As himself:) No, not you sir. Please, come in.
(As Plum:) Then, Professor Plum.
(As Scarlett:) Miss Scarlett.

> *(He hits a gong, surprising the* GUESTS.*)*

(As Cook:) Then, dinner is served.
(As Plum:) Well, that was more like a cocktail minute.
(As himself:) To the Dining Room!

> *(He moves. The* GUESTS *follow.)*

(As Cook:) Shark's fin soup.
(As Peacock, slurping:) Ooo. Yummy yum yum. My favourite!

> *(Adding in dinner table actions as needed.)*

(As himself:) Then Mr Boddy arrived and we all went to the Study.

> *(He moves in a circle around the* GUESTS.*)*

(As Yvette:) Coffee? Brandy? Sacre bleu.
(As Scarlett:) Who is this Mr Boddy, butler?
(As Boddy:) How d'you do?
(As himself:) Then Mr Boddy asked me to pass out packages.

> *(He 'passes' out packages swiftly.)*

(As White:) Ahhh! A snake! No. It's a Rope.
(As himself:) Then Mr Boddy switched off the lights.

(As Boddy:) Now! Ah! Bang! Ah!

> *(He switches off the lights. Lights go black. They scream!)*
>
> *(Lights up.* WADSWORTH *plays dead as if in a chair. They scream again!)*
>
> *(*WADSWORTH *sits up suddenly.)*

WADSWORTH. Mr Boddy was dead. But not really. Really he was alive. But we didn't know it. Then, Mrs Peacock drank his drink . . .

> *(He drinks from Peacock's flask and spits all over the* GUESTS.*)*

(As Peacock:) Poison!

> *(He screams,* PEACOCK *screams, he screams. He slaps himself.)*

(As Scarlett:) Thank God, someone had to stop her screaming!
(As himself:) And then we heard . . .

> *(He lip-syncs to a sound cue of Yvette screaming.)*

(As himself:) To the Billiard Room! But Mrs Peacock joined late.
(As Peacock:) I'm an old woman who may or may not have been poisoned.
(As himself:) Then Mrs White asked . . .
(As White:) Who else is in the house?
(As himself:) To which we all replied . . .

ALL. *(They look out:)* ZE COOK!

> *(He moves.)*

WADSWORTH. Who we found knifed in the back!

> *(He mimes stabbing her, then imitates the Cook falling dead out of the pantry onto Green.)*

WADSWORTH. *(As Green:)* Oh God. Oh God. So upsetting. Blood. Germs. *(Muffled by his own arm:)* Will somebody help me up!
(As himself, miming dragging the Cook:) I suggested we take the Cook's body into the Study.

> *(He sits as 'dead' Boddy, then hops up, revealing a blank space!)*

(As himself:) But Boddy's body was gone!

> *(He mimes draping himself over an imaginary Peacock.)*

(As himself:) Then Mrs Peacock entered with Boddy on her body because Boddy had been bludgeoned in his bonce.

> *(Then:)*

(As himself:) Then, the briefcase!

(He mimes opening the briefcase at the desk. They gasp.)

WADSWORTH. *(As himself:)* Empty!

(Then:)

(As himself:) Next the Motorist arrived . . .
(As Mustard:) Are you a killer?
(As himself:) And I locked him in the Lounge!

> *(He fake-kills GREEN like the Motorist, with a mimed Spanner to the head. GREEN drops 'dead' à la Motorist.)*

WADSWORTH. Dead!

(He moves to the front door.)

(As himself:) That's when the unexpected Bobby showed up.
(As Bobby:) Hello . . . you're all acting rather peculiar.
(As himself:) Can you canoe?

> *(He fake-kills PLUM with a mimed Candlestick to the head — PLUM drops 'dead' à la the Bobby.)*

WADSWORTH. Dead! Then the maid got strangled in the Billiard Room!

> *(He fake-strangles SCARLETT with a mimed Rope — SCARLETT drops 'dead' à la Yvette.)*

WADSWORTH. *(As himself:)* Dead! Which brings us to . . .
(As Singing Telegram Girl:) I am . . . *(Fake shooting.)* BANG!

> *(WHITE goes down as if shot.)*

> *(EVERYONE is down except MUSTARD and PEACOCK.)*

WADSWORTH. And here we all are.

MUSTARD. *(Clapping:)* Bravo!

(As they speak, they slowly rise back up.)

WHITE. Impressive, Wadsworth.

PLUM. But what does it prove?!

GREEN. Nothing!

WADSWORTH. Well . . .

SCARLETT. *(Interrupting:)* Enough of this! I know who the murderer is!

ALL. You do?!

SCARLETT. I do!

WADSWORTH. All right then. We're listening, Miss Scarlett. Who do you accuse?

(SCARLETT *reveals Plum's pipe, pointing it at* PLUM.)

SCARLETT. It was PROFESSOR PLUM, IN THE HALL, WITH THE REVOLVER!

(*They look/gasp.*)

PLUM. Liar!

SCARLETT. We all heard the gun go off, Professor! And I found your stupid tobacco pipe here when we were searching the house. When did you drop it, huh? While seeking out the best vantage point to kill your next victim?! I bet that poor Singing Telegram Girl was an old patient of yours, correct?

PLUM. I never saw that girl before in my life! It wasn't me . . .

WADSWORTH. Well. The gun is missing. Gentlemen, turn out your pockets. Ladies, empty your purses. Whoever has the gun is the murderer.

(*They all do so.* PLUM *pulls out the Revolver with a grunt. He points it at* WADSWORTH. *The* GUESTS *gasp!*)

GREEN. Well done, Wadsworth!

PLUM. (*Threatening:*) You won't be able to prove anything if you're all dead!

WADSWORTH. That may be so, Professor Plum. (*With condescending confidence as he crosses to the front door:*) But if we're alive . . .

(*He opens the door. The* POLICE INSPECTOR *and his* BACKUP OFFICER *enter, guns and ID revealed.*)

WADSWORTH. Officers. (*Pointing at* PLUM:) There's your man.

INSPECTOR. Well done, Wadsworth!

GREEN. That's what I said!

INSPECTOR. Yes, well, I'm saying it now. I'm Hank Cuffs, of Scotland Yard. (*Disarming/cuffing* PLUM:) And Professor Plum, you're coming with me.

(*Music sting. Cast freezes.* PLUM *breaks the freeze to step forwards and say . . .*)

PLUM. That's not how it happened! It happened like this . . .

(*They physically rewind—to the sound of a tape rewinding—back to their positions.*)

WADSWORTH. All right then. We're listening, Professor Plum. Who do you accuse?

(PLUM *waves Mustard's medal.*)

PLUM. It was COLONEL MUSTARD, IN THE LOUNGE, WITH THE SPANNER!

MUSTARD. I never lounge!

PLUM. I found your medal of honor in the Lounge where the Motorist was killed by a Spanner to the head; and that Spanner belongs to you!

MUSTARD. That's a lie!

WADSWORTH. The Spanner is missing. Gentlemen, turn out your pockets. Ladies, empty your purses. Whoever has the Spanner, is the murderer.

(*They all do.* MUSTARD *pulls out the Spanner with a threatening grunt.*)

(*They look/gasp! A bit faster.*)

GREEN. Well done, Wadsworth!

(POLICE *enter. Guns and ID revealed.*)

WADSWORTH. There's your man, Officer. Not a colonel of truth in him.

INSPECTOR. Well done, Wadsworth!

GREEN. That's what I said!

INSPECTOR. Yes, well, I'm saying it now. Gil T. Verdict, of Scotland Yard. (*Disarming/cuffing* MUSTARD:) Colonel Mustard, you're coming with me.

(*Music sting. Cast freezes.* MUSTARD *breaks the freeze to step forwards and say . . .*)

MUSTARD. You have it all wrong! It happened like this . . .

(*They physically rewind—to the sound of a tape rewinding—a bit faster now . . .*)

WADSWORTH. We're listening, Colonel. Who do you accuse?

(MUSTARD *holds high White's veil.*)

MUSTARD. It was MRS WHITE, IN THE BILLIARD ROOM, WITH THE ROPE!

(*They look/gasp!*)

WHITE. I'd rather die!

MUSTARD. I found your veil in the Billiard Room! And I saw how you cringed tonight when Yvette served you dinner.

WHITE. Yes, it's true, I knew Yvette . . . she had a torrid love affair with my late husband. I hated her. I hated her SO MUCH. It . . . it . . . the . . . FLAMES. On the side of my face. Breathing. HEAVING . . . breaths . . . But just because I hated her, doesn't mean I killed her!

WADSWORTH. The Rope is missing. Gentlemen, turn out your pockets. Ladies . . .

> (WHITE *pulls out the Rope with a yelp. They gasp as she waves it threateningly.*)

GREEN. Well done, Wadsworth!

> (POLICE *burst in, faster now.*)

INSPECTOR. *(Nearly at the same time:)* Well done, Wadsworth!

GREEN. That's what I said!

INSPECTOR. *(Nearly at the same time:)* Yes, well, I'm saying it now. Mark M'Words, of Scotland Yard. *(Disarming/cuffing* WHITE:*)* Mrs White . . .

> (*Music sting. Faster now . . . Before they even have time to freeze,* WHITE *shouts . . .*)

WHITE. It happened like this . . .

> (*They rewind – to the sound of a tape rewinding – even faster now.*)

WADSWORTH. Mrs White, who do you accuse?

> (*They barely have time to rewind back to position.* WHITE *holds Peacock's feather . . .*)

WHITE. It was MRS PEACOCK, IN THE KITCHEN, WITH THE DAGGER! I found your feather by the corpse!

WADSWORTH. Gentlemen, turn out your pockets . . .

> (PEACOCK *reveals a Dagger with a shout.*)

GREEN/INSPECTOR. Well done, Wadsworth!

> (POLICE *enter on* GREEN's *line, disarming and cuffing* PEACOCK.)

GREEN/INSPECTOR. That's what I said! Yes, well, I'm saying it now.

INSPECTOR. I'm Barry D. Hatchett.

ALL. Of Scotland Yard!

PEACOCK. But that's not how it happened!

ALL. IT HAPPENED LIKE THIS!

(They physically rewind too quickly even for the sound cue . . .)

PEACOCK. It was MISS SCARLETT, IN THE LIBRARY, WITH THE CANDLESTICK!

(Before anyone can say anything . . .)

INSPECTOR Max E. Mumm, of Scotland Yard.

SCARLETT. *(To* WADSWORTH*:)* You can't do this to me!

WADSWORTH. Frankly, Miss Scarlett, I don't give a damn.

(Music sting.)

(Then, WADSWORTH *breaks the freeze and steps forwards.)*

WADSWORTH. But—it really happened like this.

(They do one final [irritated/lackluster] rewind.)

WADSWORTH. I know who the murderer is.

ALL. Who?!

WADSWORTH. All of you!

(They gasp!)

WADSWORTH. Hands up!

*(*WADSWORTH *reveals a gun.)*

WADSWORTH. Nobody move! You're all killers!

SCARLETT. You can't prove anything, Mr Wadsworth!

WADSWORTH. I'm not Mr Wadsworth. *(In Boddy's aristrocratic accent:)* I'm Mr Boddy!

PEACOCK. How can you be Mr Boddy if Boddy bled all over me!

WADSWORTH. It wasn't Boddy who was bleeding.

MUSTARD. But if the body wasn't Boddy . . . then who was he?

WADSWORTH. *He* was Wadsworth. My butler.

(They gasp.)

WADSWORTH. And that's not all chaps . . . *(Now with an American accent:)* I ain't exactly who I seem!

ALL. An AMERICAN!!!!

(This is clearly worse than being a killer. They all talk together, ad lib, e.g.:)

MUSTARD. Now look here sir, you can't just impersonate a gentleman . . . /

WHITE. How vulgar and plebian . . . /

PLUM. Overpaid, oversexed and over here! /

GREEN. You vile, filthy Judas! /

WADSWORTH. Freeze! All of you . . .

SCARLETT. *(Shutting them up and stopping* WADSWORTH:*)* *WAIT!!!!* But how come you came to be here? In an English manor house?

WADSWORTH. I bought it off some hard-up posh guy by the name of Black. When I say bought . . . his body's in the cellar.

MUSTARD. Mr Boddy is in the cellar now?

ALL. *(Beyond irritated:)* Mr Black is the body in the cellar.

SCARLETT. *(Pointing at* WADSWORTH:*)* HE is Mr Boddy.

MUSTARD. Yes of course, I see.

(He doesn't.)

SCARLETT. But if you're the real Mr Boddy, what was your purpose in dragging this all out?

WADSWORTH. Well, when you started murdering people, I decided to roll the dice. See if you'd self-implode. Kill off my entire network of spies and informers. Which you all did, splendidly, by the way. Generously leaving your fingerprints on every glass, doorknob, and . . . dead body. So, now I have each of you on the hook for murder!

PEACOCK. Murder?!

WADSWORTH. Bribery for petty crimes is one thing . . . but murder? Now that could get expensive.

WHITE. But why this whole charade?!

PEACOCK. The searching of the house, the madness of retracing our steps?!

WADSWORTH. It's all part of the game!

ALL. Game?!

WADSWORTH. Well, yeah, I'm relaxed now, you see. Now that you've killed everyone off—there's no evidence left against me. I've got off . . . scot-free.

PLUM. But the police will be here any minute. You'll never get away with this!

(WADSWORTH laughs knowingly.)

MUSTARD. What's so funny?

SCARLETT. Nobody's called the police have they?

WHITE. They were never on their way.

WADSWORTH. Now, listen up, you reprobates. We're gonna stack the bodies in the cellar, lock the cellar door, leave Boddy Manor one at a time, and forget that any of this ever happened.

PLUM. I can't forget all this!

WADSWORTH. With murder on the menu, the price of blackmail just tripled!

PLUM. Forgotten!

WADSWORTH. Now move!

SCARLETT. Wait a minute! We can all rush him. He's got no more bullets left in that gun.

WADSWORTH. Oh, come on, you don't think I'm gonna fall for that old trick.

SCARLETT. It's not a trick. *(She holds up her fingers:)* There was one shot at Mr Boddy in the Study, two for the chandelier, two at the Lounge door and one for the Singing Telegram Girl.

WADSWORTH. That's not six.

SCARLETT. One plus two plus two plus one.

WADSWORTH. Uh-uh. There was only one shot that got the chandelier, that's one plus two plus ONE plus one.

SCARLETT. Even if you were right, that would be one plus one, plus two plus one, not one plus two plus one plus one.

WADSWORTH. Okay fine. One plus two plus—SHUT UP! Point is, there is one bullet left in this gun, and anybody who moves is gonna get it!

GREEN. So, you're just going to keep blackmailing us and we're all supposed to pretend this never happened?

WADSWORTH. Of course. Why not?

GREEN. I'll tell you why not ... Lawrence Goodman! Of SCOTLAND YARD!

(He draws a gun.)

GREEN. The jig, as you Americans say, is up!

(They gasp [except WADSWORTH].)

WADSWORTH. Or is it?!

(WADSWORTH turns and shoots GREEN! GREEN dodges with Matrix-esque finesse.)

GREEN. *(Smugly:)* Missed me.

(GREEN trains his gun on WADSWORTH, who is genuinely now frightened.)

MUSTARD. You're SCOTLAND YARD?!

GREEN. Apparently I'm a dead-ringer for Green. He got a letter just like each of you. But he came to the Yard to ask for help. I took his place tonight so we could have a sting operation.

PEACOCK. Some sting! Six people died on your watch!

GREEN. I usually work in the backroom, at a desk... *(Then, recovering his bravado:)* My beat is property crime—you know theft, fraud. That's why I was so tickled when the real Mr Wadsworth risked his neck to drop off a whole briefcase worth of evidence last night.

PLUM. You've had the evidence this whole time?!

GREEN. *(Referencing his whole body.)* It's all here.

ALL. What?

GREEN. *(Pulling from a pocket:)* Miss Scarlet's books—including client names and dates of 'service,' proving she's one of Soho's top madams and justifying why she killed the poor Bobby—who's listed here, on her payroll.

SCARLETT. Give me that!

(SCARLETT lunges at GREEN. He staves her off with his gun.)

GREEN. *(Pulling from another pocket:)* Ooo, and a love letter addressed to Professor Plum...

PLUM. That's private property!

GREEN. That Singing Telegram Girl was the underage daughter of the head of the U-NO WHO, *who* would have come clean to Pater—who would have cleaned out Professor Plum. So, you killed her.

PLUM. Now see here...

(WADSWORTH makes an attempt to escape—GREEN trains the gun on him again, grounding him.)

GREEN. *(To WADSWORTH:)* Ah-ah-aaah!... *(Now to MUSTARD—trying to pull negatives out of his sock:)* And these negatives... *(He can't* *pull them out so he tries again.)* And these negati ... *(One more time — success.)* And these negatives, Colonel. Quite the regular at Miss Scarlet's 'establishment.' But you couldn't be a Colonel anymore if that Motorist had informed your General where he drives you on Tuesday nights.

MUSTARD. I just wanted somebody to talk with!

> *(WADSWORTH takes a step towards GREEN's gun. GREEN thwarts his attempt with ninja-like moves and carries on with a flourish.)*

GREEN. Shark's fin soup indeed, Mrs Peacock. Too bad your old Cook couldn't keep quiet. If only she hadn't gabbed about your briberies, maybe you wouldn't have killed her — just before joining us outside the Billiard Room. Now we know what really took you so long.

PEACOCK. Circumstantial evidence will never hold up in a court of law!

GREEN. *(Unzipping his pants and pulling it out from his crotch:)* But this affidavit from the Cook will. *(Off of* PEACOCK's *disgusted reaction, now to* WHITE.*)* And Mrs White ... *(He zips his fly.)* ... You weren't lying, were you? You really did hate Yvette.

WHITE. *(Reprising her moment:)* Flames ... flames on the side —

GREEN. Calm yourself madam, we 'get it' as Mr Boddy would say. *(Revealing a vial, seemingly out of thin air:)* Here's a container holding fingerprints collected at the scenes of your previous murders —

WHITE. I never murdered my husbands!

GREEN. Fingerprints I'm sure Scotland Yard will be able to match to those found on the noose tied around Yvette's neck.

WHITE. I wore gloves!

GREEN. *(Tearing open his vest to reveal White's gloves pinned to his chest:)* You mean these?

> *(WHITE turns away à la 'Damn.')*

GREEN. And last, but not least, Mr Bobby Boddy.

WADSWORTH. It's Robert.

GREEN. Now *you* didn't hate Yvette at all, did you Mr Boddy?

WADSWORTH. What's it to you?

GREEN. 'Illicit American/Franco/South Londoner love affair' is the icing on the cake of this file. For one reason only ... You loved her.

> *(WADSWORTH sheds a tear ...)*

GREEN. A Scotland Yard file on the whole Boddy family. Your butler, the real Wadsworth, has been feeding us information for months. Talk about a real American patriot.

WADSWORTH. He was British.

GREEN. Exactly!

(EVERYONE is confused. GREEN is triumphant.)

ALL. What?

(Then:)

GREEN. I see why you would want to kill him. Twice. Your shot missed him in the Study. But he wisely played dead. And it wasn't until you caught him trying to escape that you bludgeoned him to death with the Lead Pipe I'd dropped on my way to the Kitchen.

PLUM. *(To* SCARLETT:*)* I mean really, who drops a murder weapon?

GREEN. *(Defensive:)* I didn't know it was a . . . *(Back to brass tacks:)* The Boddy family has been wanted for organised crime on both sides of the Atlantic for generations but they've always eluded the law. Until now. Tonight, the 'Boddy Business' has reached a dead end.

WADSWORTH. You leave my family out of this!

(WADSWORTH, enraged, uses the Dagger he's snagged from Peacock's purse to lunge at GREEN . . .)

(GREEN fires, shooting WADSWORTH successfully! EVERYONE gasps!)

WADSWORTH. Ow! Owwww! *(Dying – free-form loose improvisation here – falling into GREEN's arms.)* Oh, Larry. Oh I can taste the lead. Hold me Larry.

GREEN. It's Lawrence.

WADSWORTH. Oh, it's so dark. *(Then:)* False alarm! *(He's back up – maybe with a tap dance and song.)* 'If I knew you were coming, I'd have baked you a cake!' *(Then – down again, clutching his heart – finally dying with great dramatic flare.)* Ow. Ow. Ow. Ow. I'm really going now. Oh yes, this is it. The end of my days. Oh the pain. Goodbye cruel world. I'm going. I'm going. I'm going. I'm going. I'm going. I'm going. I'm going. I'm going. Going. Still going. Going. Gone.

(He appears dead.)

PLUM. He's dead!

WADSWORTH. *(Back up again:)* Not yet.

(They all gasp!)

PLUM. *(Disappointed in himself:)* God!

WADSWORTH. *(Singing:)* 'Smile, when your heart is breaking . . . smile . . . ' *(Then in pain:)* Mama! *(Crawling across the stage towards GREEN:)* Larry. Larrrrry. I see the light Larry. A big, big, bright light. Shining down on me Larry. The angels are guiding me to the light Larry. Larry had a little lamb. Little lamb. Little lamb. Larry. Feed my goldfish Larry. Hold my hand Larry. Larry. Larry. Larry. Larry. *(One final death rattle:)* Larry . . .

GREEN. *(Very quietly.)* Lawrence . . .

(WADSWORTH groans and dies.)

GREEN. I don't mind telling you, this was the most exciting night I've had in a long time.

ALL. What?

(Then:)

GREEN. And now, you're all under arrest. *(Towards the front door:)* Officers . . .

(POLICE with the INSPECTOR burst through the front door. The GUESTS hold up their hands.)

GREEN. Here are the criminals you've been looking for and you'll find the recordings of the confessions we've been waiting for in the Billiard Room.

PLUM. *(Doh!)* The tapes!

INSPECTOR. All right. Whodunit?

ALL. *(Each pointing at one of the others:)* He/she did!

GREEN. They all did! But if you want to know who killed Mr Boddy . . . *(Indicates WADSWORTH.)* It was me. Desk Sergeant Lawrence Goodman, in the Hall, with my pistol.

INSPECTOR. Well done, Goodman.

ALL. That's what he said!

GREEN. *(Arrogantly twirling his gun:)* Alright Inspector take them away! I'm going home to have relations with my wife.

(His gun goes off! GREEN accidentally shoots the POLICE. EVERYONE SCREAMS!)

GREEN. Sorry. Sorry.

End of Play

No one shall make any changes in this title for the purpose of production. No part of this book may be reproduced, stored in a retrieval system, scanned, uploaded, or transmitted in any form, by any means, now known or yet to be invented, including mechanical, electronic, digital, photocopying, recording, videotaping, or otherwise, without the prior written permission of the publisher. No one shall share this title, or part of this title, to any social media or file hosting websites.

The moral right of Jonathan Lynn and Sandy Rustin to be identified as authors of this work has been asserted in accordance with Section 77 of the Copyright, Designs and Patents Act 1988.

USE OF COPYRIGHTED MUSIC

A licence issued by Concord Theatricals to perform this play does not include permission to use the incidental music specified in this publication. In the United Kingdom: Where the place of performance is already licensed by the PERFORMING RIGHT SOCIETY (PRS) a return of the music used must be made to them. If the place of performance is not so licensed then application should be made to PRS for Music (www.prsformusic.com). A separate and additional licence from PHONOGRAPHIC PERFORMANCE LTD (www. ppluk.com) may be needed whenever commercial recordings are used. Outside the United Kingdom: Please contact the appropriate music licensing authority in your territory for the rights to any incidental music.

USE OF COPYRIGHTED THIRD-PARTY MATERIALS

Licensees are solely responsible for obtaining formal written permission from copyright owners to use copyrighted third-party materials (e.g., artworks, logos) in the performance of this play and are strongly cautioned to do so. If no such permission is obtained by the licensee, then the licensee must use only original materials that the licensee owns and controls. Licensees are solely responsible and liable for clearances of all third-party copyrighted materials, and shall indemnify the copyright owners of the play(s) and their licensing agent, Concord Theatricals Ltd., against any costs, expenses, losses and liabilities arising from the use of such copyrighted third-party materials by licensees.

IMPORTANT BILLING AND CREDIT REQUIREMENTS

If you have obtained performance rights to this title, please refer to your licensing agreement for important billing and credit requirements.

www.ingramcontent.com/pod-product-compliance
Ingram Content Group UK Ltd.
Pitfield, Milton Keynes, MK11 3LW, UK
UKHW020137190126
467113UK00001B/3